Y0-BQX-016

TALES OF TWO CITIES

cross-border talks

TALES OF TWO CITIES

KULDIP NAYAR

ASIF NOORANI

SERIES EDITOR
DAVID PAGE

LOTUS COLLECTION
ROLI BOOKS

Lotus Collection

© Kuldip Nayar and Asif Noorani, 2008

This edition published in 2008
The Lotus Collection
An imprint of Roli Books Pvt. Ltd.
M-75, G.K. II Market, New Delhi 110 048
Phones: ++91 (011) 2921 2271, 2921 2782
2921 0886, Fax: ++91 (011) 2921 7185
E-mail: roli@vsnl.com; Website: rolibooks.com
Also at
Varanasi, Bangalore, Kolkata, Jaipur, Chennai & Mumbai

Cover design: Supriya Saran
Layout design: Narendra Shahi

ISBN: 978-81-7436-676-4

Typeset in AGaramond by Roli Books Pvt. Ltd. and
printed at Rekmo Printers, Okhla, New Delhi.

To Our Parents

this stained light, this night-bitten dawn –
this is not the dawn we yearned for.
this is not the dawn
for which we set out so eagerly.

– From *The Morning of Freedom*
by Faiz Ahmed Faiz *(Tr. by Daud Kamal)*

contents

introduction   1
david page

from sialkot to delhi   13
kuldip nayar

from bombay to karachi   71
asif noorani

introduction

'It was the best of times, it was the worst of times, it was the age of wisdom, it was the age of foolishness, it was the epoch of belief, it was the epoch of incredulity, it was the season of Light, it was the season of Darkness, it was the spring of hope, it was the winter of despair, we had everything before us, we had nothing before us …'

With these famous words, Charles Dickens began *A Tale of Two Cities*, which is set in Paris and London at the time of the French Revolution of 1789, one of the biggest social and political upheavals in modern European history.

The words might equally apply to events in the subcontinent in 1947, to the division of Britain's Indian Empire into the two states of India and Pakistan and the accompanying disturbances and mass migration. Independence brought with it great hope for the future on both sides of the new borders but it was also undoubtedly the worst of times and a season of darkness, as hundreds of thousands of people were killed in communal disturbances and millions left their homes and their livelihoods for an uncertain future in a new country.

Tales of Two Cities sets out to tell that story – of independence, of upheaval and migration and of new beginnings – through the eyes of two observers, whose families were uprooted and who were forced to start new lives in new states in those unpropitious circumstances.

Kuldip Nayar, one of India's most eminent journalists, was twenty-four years old in 1947 when his father had to abandon his solid medical practice in the town of Sialkot and the family sought refuge with relatives in Delhi. They had initially decided to remain in Pakistan after Independence and were strengthened in their resolve by the assurances given to the minorities by Muhammed Ali Jinnah, Pakistan's first governor-general. However, on Pakistan's Independence Day, 14 August, fear gripped the Hindu community in Sialkot so suddenly that the family got up from their lunch and left behind almost everything they owned. After a spell with friends in the neighbouring cantonment, they set off for Delhi, hoping to return once the situation normalized. But it was not to be.

Asif Noorani, distinguished Pakistani journalist and critic, was only five years old at Partition. He remembers the riots in Bombay and was aware of some horrific incidents in his neighbourhood. But the family weathered that storm and lived in Bombay for three more years before his father decided to migrate to Pakistan in search of work. His father's business partner, the major shareholder in the medical store in Bombay where he worked, had already left for Pakistan and when his stake was taken over by a Hindu migrant from Sindh, Asif's father saw the writing on the wall. This was in fact a case of economic migration, undertaken with some reluctance, triggered by changing patterns of business ownership, and to a greater extent a matter of choice rather than compulsion. As Asif himself writes: 'Even those who were not in favour of Partition migrated to Pakistan in search of better opportunities.'

Kuldip Nayar's tale graphically reflects the extraordinary scenes in Punjab, where communities, which had lived alongside each other for generations, suddenly found that harmony and trust had been replaced by communal hatred and killing. On his journey from Sialkot to Lahore along the Grand Trunk Road, Kuldip witnessed a sea of humanity on the move in both directions. He saw death and destruction on the roadside and heard harrowing stories from enraged and impoverished refugees trying to preserve life and limb, despite the woeful breakdown of law and order. Later, after crossing the new border, he even came close to being killed himself on suspicion of being a Muslim.

Estimates of the scale of the killing and migration vary but the enormity of what happened is not in doubt. In Punjab particularly, there was a wholesale transfer of populations, which amounted in effect to ethnic cleansing. Virtually all Sikhs and Hindus migrated or were expelled from West Punjab and almost all Muslims were forced out of the eastern districts of the province. The city of Lahore, former capital of Ranjit Singh's kingdom and a great centre of Sikh culture, became within a matter of months an exclusively Muslim city, while in Delhi, the capital of a succession of Muslim Empires, many Muslim families packed their bags and left for Pakistan. It was an irony of the times that the great Red Fort, which Shah Jahan had built as a symbol of Mughal power, now became a refuge for Delhi's own Muslim community until passions cooled and order was restored.

The unbounded ferocity witnessed in Punjab was exceptional. Bengal did not see the same thorough-going transfers of populations, nor did Muslim minority provinces such as the United Provinces (now Uttar Pradesh), Bihar, or the Central Provinces (now Madhya Pradesh) from which the Muslim middle class

migrated in huge numbers to the urban centres of Sindh. Across the
whole of India, Muslims were under considerable pressure to opt for
Pakistan but outside Punjab, many remained behind and migration
was more voluntary and orderly.

Bombay, the commercial capital of India, from which Asif
Noorani's family set sail for Pakistan in 1950, was to provide some
of the leading entrepreneurs of the new state, who helped to make
Karachi its financial and industrial centre as well as its first capital.
Strong links already existed between the two cities, which had been
part of the same Bombay Presidency until Sindh became a separate
province in 1936. Muhammed Ali Jinnah, the was a Karachiite by
birth, who migrated to Bombay to make his name as a lawyer after
qualifying for the bar in London. His own return to Karachi in
1947 was perhaps the most significant migration of all, though it
was symptomatic of his strong feeling for Bombay that he retained
his house on Malabar Hill and fully intended to retire there before
the Partition massacres and his own terminal illness made that
impossible.

The *Tales of Two Cities* offered by Kuldip Nayar and Asif
Noorani reflect these very different Partition experiences. Kuldip's
migration from Sialkot to Delhi across the ethnically cleansed plains
of Punjab was a very different experience from Asif Noorani's family
passage from Bombay to Karachi in 1950 on board the *S.S.
Sabarmati*, a regular steamer service which continued to run until
the 1965 war.

Their accounts of pre-Partition society and culture naturally
reflect their age and circumstances at the time. Coming from what
he calls 'a secular-minded family of practising Muslims', the young
Asif Noorani seems to have been almost unconscious of other
religious communities, assuming that Hindu school friends at his

kindergarten must also be Muslims of some sort. Kuldip Nayar, on the other hand, had already graduated from the Law College at Lahore, had questioned Mr Jinnah in a public meeting and had heard Maulana Abul Kalam Azad point out the potential pitfalls of Partition for the Muslim community. He was a politically conscious young man and had formed a peace committee with his friends in Sialkot to help preserve good relations between the communities.

Both authors convey a similar sense of paradise lost, of harmony destroyed, not by those who had lived peaceably side by side with each other for years but by provocation from outside. In Sialkot particularly, it was the arrival of Muslim refugees from other parts of Punjab, imbued with hatred of those who had expelled them, which triggered the collapse of cordiality and trust and provoked the forced migration of Hindus and Sikhs from the town.

Kuldip Nayar's tale provides both a personal account of his family's migration and some remarkable vignettes from the politics of the period. As a young journalist, he reported the assassination of Mahatma Gandhi in January 1948, heard Nehru speak at Birla House of his own sense of the nation's loss, observed Nehru, Patel, Baldev Singh and Mountbatten in conclave after the event, and wept himself at what it meant for India.

It is no small tribute to Kuldip's transparent secularism that as a young Hindu migrant he was taken on as a tyro journalist by a Muslim paper based in Old Delhi. He was later to become Resident Editor of the *Statesman*, one of India's leading English dailies, but he began his career in the Urdu language newspaper, *Anjam*, published in Old Delhi's Muslim heartland. Here, in the narrow lanes between Daryaganj and the Jama Masjid, he was able to observe Muslims in shock as they tried to deal with the consequences of Pakistan and the division of the Indian Muslim community by the new and hurriedly drawn boundary. This was the beginning of some difficult years for India's Muslims, whose loyalty had become suspect and whose language and culture had become associated with another state.

Asif Noorani spent his first years in Pakistan as a schoolboy in Lahore, where his father began work with his former business partner on the promise of a similar relationship. The family took up residence in a bungalow in Model Town, the most modern, spacious and green suburb in the city. Most of the bungalows had been built by prosperous Hindus and Sikhs who had left their homes just as suddenly as Kuldip Nayar's family left Sialkot, only to be replaced almost immediately by Muslim families fleeing from harassment and death in East Punjab. The knife-edge uncertainty of those days added to the sense of crisis. It was not until just after Independence that the Radcliffe Award made it clear that Lahore would be a part of Pakistan.

Kuldip Nayar laments the destruction of the old composite culture of Punjab, in which Hindus, Sikhs and Muslims had shared a love of Urdu and of Persian and been educated side by side in the same colleges and schools. The land of the five rivers, with its magnificent irrigation systems, which was ruled for so long by the Punjab Unionist party, representing all three communities, had become a land of divided communities and divided waterways. It was one thing to draw the line; it was quite another to deal with the severing of age-old relationships and long established patterns of trade and communication.

Since Partition, as a believer in 'cooperation, not confrontation', Kuldip has actively maintained his links with friends in Pakistan, like the poet Faiz Ahmed Faiz, who also came from Sialkot and whose famous poem, *The Morning of Freedom*, both authors have chosen to begin this book. But despite the progress of recent years, he fears that succeeding generations of Punjabis, who have grown up divided from each other and without a common allegiance to Urdu, will neither realize what has been lost nor be so concerned to repair the damage.

Asif Noorani is more confident of cultural continuities. As a music and film enthusiast and the former editor of a film magazine, he has maintained strong links with friends and fellow professionals in Bombay, whose cultural industry continues to wield enormous influence across Asia and Africa. His tale testifies to the enduring popularity of Bollywood among audiences in Pakistan, and particularly among the Urdu speaking communities of Karachi. Indian cinema remains a powerful source of secular values, with its handsome complement of stars from all communities, speaking a popular form of Urdu, which is still better understood as a South Asian lingua franca than some of the more highly developed national languages.

These perceptions of continuity and discontinuity are also evident from the accounts, which both authors give of their visits to their birthplaces after Independence. Kuldip Nayar's brief return to Sialkot in 1972, shortly after the hostilities which led to the creation of Bangladesh, is a desolate experience for him. Many of the places are recognizably the same but he no longer has any connection with the town. The wounds inflicted by Partition are still too painful for him to want to stay for long. His feeling for his birthplace had undergone an irrevocable change.

Asif Noorani, on the other hand, began revisiting Bombay not long after Partition and has continued to do so ever since. He still has some family members living here and the pull of old friendships remains strong. His accounts of two of his early visits to India – in

1964 and 1965 – provide lively and entertaining insights into the problems of travel for divided Muslim families and the distorted perceptions of life in the other country which have stood in the way of easy access and understanding for more than half a century. These distortions, which have been removed to some extent by the growth of satellite television, are well illustrated by Asif's experience as a young Pakistani marooned in Bombay during the 1965 war. His family feared that he had been interned but he was in fact spending his time going to the cinema with his friends and relatives.

Despite their different perceptions, both authors write with equal persuasion about the urban transformation of their adopted cities after 1947. Kuldip Nayar gives an amusingly self-deprecating account of the impact of the arrival of so many Punjabis on what he calls the 'dainty, decent culture' of Delhi. The city's Muslims, already on the defensive, were soon overwhelmed by the thousands of dynamic and resourceful urban professionals and businessmen who arrived from Lahore and other towns of Punjab. One of the first places they settled was Karol Bagh, where Kuldip's family set up their new home, but before long many new colonies sprang up to accommodate the migrants and much of South Delhi became an area of Punjabi settlement. 'Delhi was all Punjab in the fifties, sixties and early seventies,' writes Kuldip.

The transformation of Karachi was no less dramatic. Before Partition, Karachi was known as one of the neatest and cleanest of India's cities. With a population of less than half a million and an attractive coastal location, it was a city where the Sindhi Hindu middle class was the dominant community, whether in the professions or in trade. Things began to change after 1936, when Karachi became the capital of the newly created province of Sindh, but with Partition and the decision to make Karachi the capital of

Pakistan, the floodgates opened and hundreds of thousands of Mohajirs from India's Muslim minority provinces poured in, overwhelming the local administration and posing an enormous housing challenge. Asif Noorani tells the story of the creation of the new Karachi with a fine eye for detail: the sense of resilience and mutual support among the new arrivals, the emergence of new suburbs like Nazimabad and PECHS, and the continued attachment of the Mohajirs to their places of origin, which was illustrated by the names they chose for their shops and businesses.

The fact that the capitals of India and Pakistan became cities dominated by their refugee populations undoubtedly influenced the state of relations between the two countries after Independence. In both countries, these were powerful constituencies whose experience at the hands of the other community left a residue of hostility which helped to deepen the divide which Partition had begun. 'A few weeks of madness,' writes Kuldip Nayar 'embittered relations between the two countries for generations to come.'

The effects were most keenly felt among those Muslims families who had migrated to Pakistan and found themselves divided from their relatives in India by the new borders. Asif Noorani's emphasis on the problems of obtaining permits and visas and the need for the Indian government to re-open its consulate in Karachi points up the difficulties these families continue to face.

Kuldip Nayar's experience of Partition turned him into a life-long campaigner for better relations between the two countries. He regularly writes about India and Pakistan in his syndicated columns and has produced two books on the subject, *Distant Neighbours: A Tale of the Subcontinent*, published in 1973, and *Wall at Wagah: India-Pakistan Relations*, which came out thirty years later. He remains haunted by the events of 1947 and has attempted through his own investigations to discover how the division took place and whether the bloodshed could have been avoided. His interview with Lord Radcliffe, the chairman of the Boundary Commission, conducted in his flat in London in 1971, which is included in this volume, makes plain the magnitude of the task he faced in determining the border. Radcliffe was working against the clock, with relatively scanty information and without much confidence in his Indian colleagues, who were themselves divided on communal lines. But Kuldip's portrayal of the eminent jurist drawing lines across countryside he was not able to visit, while others experienced communal mayhem on the Grand Trunk Road, is both surreal and disturbing, raising important questions about the British responsibility for the way that Partition took place.

In recent years, Karachi and Delhi have both become megacities with all the attendant problems of overcrowding, pollution and crime. The Mohajirs remain dominant politically in Karachi but that dominance is increasingly threatened by mass migration from other parts of Pakistan. Punjabi dominance of Delhi has also been diluted as the city's boundaries have expanded ever outwards and economic migrants from poorer parts of India have flooded in. Kuldip Nayar highlights the challenges to the environment posed by human greed and inadequate governance. Asif Noorani, on the other hand, is more pre-occupied with issue of security and very thankful that the terrible troubles of the 1990s, when Karachi became a battle zone between warring political factions, have now been left behind. In the last analysis, he admires the resilience of the city and its inhabitants and feels at home in Karachi because, despite its chequered political history, it exhibits the same cosmopolitanism for which he admires Bombay.

Tales of Two Cities is the fourth volume to be published in the series *Cross-Border Talks* in which eminent Indians and Pakistanis systematically discuss the issues which divide them within the covers of one book. The series is published simultaneously in India and Pakistan in order to generate discussion in both countries at the same time.

The first volume in the series looked at the *Diplomatic Divide* between the two countries since the time of the Simla Agreement. The next two volumes – *Divided by Democracy* and *Fault Lines of Nationhood* – examined the broader themes of democracy and nationalism and their role in shaping the two states and influencing their relations. These early volumes all dealt with the high politics of relations between the two countries. This volume breaks new ground in providing personal perspectives on the events of 1947 and their extraordinarily far-reaching consequences for communities in both countries. 'This was the biggest migration of people in history,' writes Kuldip Nayar, 'but no-one had anticipated it.'

Recent histories of Partition like Urvashi Butalia's *The Other Side of Silence* have begun to put ordinary people back into the picture and to show more clearly the human price of the lines that were drawn. It is a trend in historiography and literature which reflects a wider feeling in both countries that the enduring rift between them will only be healed if people to people understanding is improved. Kuldip Nayar and Asif Noorani have both been part of that process as advocates of greater contact and better relations between the two countries and their *Tales of Two Cities* are offered in the same spirit.

David Page
May 2008

from sialkot to delhi

kuldip nayar

I did not want to leave Sialkot. This was my home. I was born and brought up here. Why could not I, a Hindu, live in the Islamic state of Pakistan when there would be hundreds of thousands of Muslims living in India? True, religion was the basis of Partition. But then both the Congress and the Muslim League, the main political parties, had opposed the exchange of population. People could stay wherever they were. Then why on 14 August 1947 was I unwelcome at a place where my forefathers and their forefathers had lived for decades?

Our family had other reasons to stay back. Most patients of my father, a medical practitioner, were Muslims. My best friend, Shafquat, with whom I had grown up, lived in Sialkot. At his mere wish I had tattooed on my right arm, the Islamic insignia – the crescent and star. I was a graduate in Persian. Pakistan had declared Urdu as its national language, with which I felt at home. We had a large property and a retinue of servants. Where would we go if we were to uproot ourselves?

Then our spiritual guardian was there. It was not a superstition but our faith that the grave in our back garden was that of a Pir who protected us and guided the family whenever it faced troubles. How could we leave the Pir? The grave was our refuge. We always found relief there. Our ma, whenever harried or harassed, or after her quarrels with our father, ran to the grave for solace. We, three brothers and one sister, bowed before the Pir every Thursday in reverence and lit an earthen lamp. It was our temple.

The people of Sialkot were mild, austere and tolerant. They were cast in a different mould. Our religions or positions in life did not distance us from one another. We numbered about a lakh: 70 per cent Muslims and 30 per cent Hindus, Sikhs and Christians. As far as I could remember, we had never experienced tension, much less communal riots. Our festivals, Diwali, Holi or Eid, were jointly celebrated and most of us walked together in mourning during Moharram. Even our businesses depended on cooperative effort. There was a mixture of owners and workers from both communities. Sports goods were the main industry and many labourers worked at home with their families to meet the orders, given piecemeal. Manufacturing surgical instruments was another business in which local people were employed. Such work had brought us together, Hindus and Muslims, in a common endeavour.

Even at the height of the agitation over the demand for Pakistan, Sialkot did not experience any tension. Every day was like any other day and business was as usual. The Muslim League had probably taken out two or three processions for separation, like the ones the Congress Party had for Independence. But there was no trouble. A few pebbles thrown into the water disturbed it for a while. Otherwise, it was placid.

Artisans or *karigars,* as they were called, were spread all over the city. But over the years, *muhallas* where only Muslims or Hindus lived had cropped up. There was no dividing line: one habitation merged into another and in some places even the walls were common. It was an easy atmosphere of conviviality. There were no exclusive Muslim or Hindu eating-places; both ate at the same restaurants. Even in other parts of the city, there was normal activity; people did not know – nor did they care – who was Muslim or who was Hindu. Women moved freely, some in burqa, some in thick *chaddar* but most with just a *dupatta*, a scarf-like cover.

Most of the population was from the lower middle class, sharing each other's grief, talking about children and the elders. We would debate the demand for Pakistan many a time, but never went beyond a heated discussion. We felt we had to live together, although we had begun to think in terms of separate identity.

There was a burst of happiness when Pakistan came into being. The Muslim population was on top of the world. The Sikhs were depressed. But most people took the whole thing in their stride. The atmosphere deteriorated only when Muslims ousted from India began pouring in and when it dawned on the Muslim population that they now had an independent country of their own.

Yet there was no tension, not even a twinge of enmity. We spoke the same Punjabi. The Punjabi we spoke in Sialkot had a peculiar accent. I discovered this when I met Nawaz Sharif, then chief minister of Punjab, for the first time in Delhi in the 1990s. It took him no time to tell that I was from Sialkot. He said that the way I spoke Punjabi had a distinctive twang, a kind of accent, which was confined to the Sialkotees. I was in good company: the two great modern Urdu poets, Mohammed Iqbal and Faiz Ahmed Faiz, who were from Sialkot, spoke Punjabi in the same way. I had heard Iqbal one day at his *muhalla*, Imambara, where Shafquat had taken me. I was a child then and I never went near him out of fear. Even otherwise I would not have approached him at that time because he was speaking angrily in Punjabi. All that I remembered about him was his huge girth, sitting on a *charpai* (string bed), which almost touched the ground because of his weight.

Faiz Ahmed Faiz, the other renowned Urdu poet, became my good friend, but after Partition we never met at Sialkot. Probably the best of the Sialkotees flourished outside Sialkot. Faiz spoke Punjabi with the Sialkotee accent. He was touchy about his Urdu pronunciation, which was made fun of in Urdu circles, and he told me that he gave up Urdu poetry for some time to switch over to Punjabi. He once made a much-talked about trip to Lucknow to meet the poet, Majaz Lukhnawi, who would say '*Ji han*' (yes please), while Faiz replied '*Han ji, Han ji*', in the typical way Punjabis say 'yes'.

Poets may be seen as saints but real saints are different. Our city had honoured the visit of Guru Nanak Dev, founder of the Sikh religion. He was on his way to Medina and stopped at Sialkot for a night. A gurudwara was built many years later to celebrate his visit. Hundreds of years before Partition, Puran Bhagat, a well-known devotee of Guru Nanak, came to our city and healed many sick people. We had dug a well in his memory. But the city also had its ugly side. There was a famous story, part of the local folklore, of a dutiful son, Shravan Kumar, who became defiant when he entered Sialkot. The city had such an effect on him that on his arrival he asked his blind parents, whom he had hauled across India for months, to pay him for his labour.

Yet Sialkot's innate goodness asserted itself at the time of Partition. Some anxiety was natural before the announcement of the Radcliffe Award, delineating the borders between India and Pakistan. But there was not a single incident of violence. Even otherwise, everyone had taken it for granted that Sialkot would be a part of Pakistan. The Jain *muhalla* in the heart of the city did not go to sleep for nights. Its fears were allayed when the Muslim localities surrounding the *muhalla* assured protection.

What disturbed the city's peace was the arrival of a blood-drenched train which had been attacked near Wazirabad, forty kilometres from Sialkot. Scores of Hindus and Sikhs travelling to Jammu, only eighteen kilometres away, had been done to death. The few who escaped were grievously injured. This one incident made many Hindus and Sikhs in Sialkot migrate to India.

Our family was yet to decide about our future. On the very eve of Partition, all of us – my parents and three brothers (our sister was already in India) – sat around the dining table to discuss our course of action.

Only a few hours earlier, Quaid-e-Azam Muhammed Ali Jinnah, founder of Pakistan, had made his famous speech to the constituent assembly: 'You are free; you are free to go to your temples; you are free to go to your mosques or to any other place of worship in this state of Pakistan. You may belong to any religion or caste or creed – that has nothing to do with the business of the state … . We are starting with this fundamental principle that we are all citizens and equal citizens of one State … . Now I think we should keep that in front of us as our ideal and you will find that in course of time, Hindus would cease to be Hindus and Muslims would cease to be Muslims, not in the religious sense, because that is the personal faith of each individual, but in the political sense as citizens of the State.'

The statement repudiated his earlier thesis that religion was the basis for nationhood. Non-Muslims were now part of the Pakistan nation. The categorical assurance made all the difference. Already vacillating, this made up our mind. We decided to stay back in Sialkot. Of course, material comforts had a lot to do with our decision. My two brothers had yet to finish their medical studies, although I had already earned my law degree from Lahore.

To reassure my family on Jinnah's pronouncement, I recalled his visit to the Law College at Lahore. This was nearly three years before Pakistan was created. In reply to my question – would Hindus and Muslims jump at each other's throats once the British left? – he had said that the bitterness and antagonism which I found at present between the two communities would go after Pakistan was constituted. The two countries would be the best of friends, as were France and Britain after hundreds of years of war. This was the lesson of history, he said.

Rajinder, my elder brother, was the only one in the family who was strongly opposed to our staying back at Sialkot. He had seen animosity building up among his Muslim classmates at Amritsar Medical College where he was studying in the final year. He said that it would be suicidal to live in Sialkot after Pakistan's formation because the Muslims would turn out Hindus and Sikhs from their houses forcibly. The police would help the Muslims to do so. To imagine that was difficult. But he was proved right. It happened that way.

My mother and younger brother, Hardip, were indifferent to our discussions. However, both tended to side with me and my father, more out of consideration than conviction. Even they did not buy Rajinder's thesis that the police would side with Muslims in throwing out Hindus from their homes. I argued that I could not contemplate any government machinery entrusted with the task of maintaining law and order siding with the mob and pushing non-Muslims out from the place where they and their forefathers had lived. My father agreed with me. That ended the matter because his was the final word.

I realized that the peace committee I had formed with Shafquat and some other Muslim and Hindu friends was inactive. We would have to take concrete steps to sustain communal harmony. However, I found that the attitude of most Muslim members had undergone a change. They found little use of peace committees after Pakistan's birth. In fact, some members turned against the peace committee and considered it a slur on the fair name of Pakistan. The committee had to be wound up.

LEAVING SIALKOT

Sialkot looked no different on Pakistan's Independence Day, 14 August. The morning was like any other morning. My father went as usual to his clinic long before we ate our breakfast. But then my brothers were on vacation while he was working. In the Trunk Bazaar, where our two-storey house stood, it was like any other day, with tongas plying with more passengers than they could carry. The pedestrians on the street were few in numbers. It was too early for the traffic to pick up its speed and noise.

My father returned around 1 pm. It was unusual. He normally came home by noon. My mother was a bit tense. 'These are not good times,' she muttered, when we heard his familiar, heavy steps on the staircase.

Munshi, the cook, was heating food and Karam, the bearer, was laying the table, when we heard a loud noise from the road below. All of us leapt to the different windows in the dining room. But we could see only the tail tail-end end of the crowd disappearing over the hump at *Ghasmandi* (the grass-market), half a furlong from our house.

From the window itself, my father inquired from a passer-by what had happened. He replied in a loud voice that a sadhu was running away and some people were chasing him.

Ignoring my mother's stern instructions not to leave the room, I ran downstairs to get more details. It turned out that some Muslim refugees, who had arrived in Sialkot a few days earlier, had spotted a saffron-clad sadhu and had pelted stones at him.

We returned to the dining table shaken. No one spoke. We avoided each other's glances. We were too disturbed and too lost in our thoughts to eat. For the first time we felt scared. I wondered whether Rajinder's prophecy that one day we would be forced to leave our home would come true. Rajinder too did not say a word but the small smile playing on his face said ' *I told you so*'.

The sadhu-incident left us cold. We feared for the future. What if there was a large-scale attack on Hindus? What would we do? Before we could sort out anything, we heard someone climbing the stairs quickly. Our first reaction was to run and close the door, but it was too late.

Arjan Das, the district jail officer, walked in. He was a family friend. 'You cannot stay here,' he said. 'This place is not safe any more. I am taking you to my house'. The same Das supervised the hanging of Mahatma Gandhi's assassin, Nathuram Godse, a few years later.

His voice was comforting. Nobody questioned him. Nor did anyone want to stay back in the house. We followed him quietly, leaving the food on the table untouched. My mother hurriedly packed a suitcase and we rushed down to the car Das was driving. It was a small vehicle and we had to sit on each other's laps to fit in.

Our neighbour, Nirmala, whom I called fatso, was probably the only one to see us depart. She lived in the house opposite and endlessly looked from her window, especially after the post-ponement of her wedding. Only a few days earlier, along with a few friends, I had decorated her house with buntings, which now hung loosely. Her marriage had to be cancelled because of the disturbances.

We saw nothing unusual on the way to the jail which was located on the outskirts of the city. We breathed a sigh of relief when the car rolled into the jail's premises and the big iron gates were shut behind us.

I asked my mother if I could return to the city to convene a meeting of the peace committee. Das was aghast at my request. My father allayed his misgivings by saying in a stern voice: 'Don't bother about him. He does not realize what is happening.'

At the time of Partition, Hindu and Muslim public servants were given the choice to serve in either of the two countries. Like most Hindu officers, Das had opted for India. In the case of Muslims, it was not much different, though some preferred to stay back in India. The movement of public servants on the basis of religion was the biggest mistake. But it was the obvious fallout of a division carried out because of religion. In the absence of government servants from their own community, the minorities felt insecure and subsequently suffered because of religious prejudice.

Das advised us to leave Pakistan as soon as we could. He had heard from his Muslim colleagues that they would allow neither Hindus nor Sikhs to stay in the city. My father and I thought that Das was panicky and exaggerated the situation. Both of us wrote him off as too pessimistic and too scared. But he turned out to be right, like my brother, Rajinder.

It seemed that some trouble had started in the afternoon of 14 August. We heard stray bullets being fired at a distance. Even the jail's thick walls could not blot out the noise. It meant that even peaceful Sialkot was not that peaceful any more. Sialkot had never seen such trouble before. We thought some outsiders must be behind it. Things would settle down. But suppose my brother's warning were to come true? We could not even think of that. Still we wondered if we would lose everything if we had to go to India. Would my father, then sixty-five years old, have to start his life all over again? My two brothers had yet to finish their studies. My father had little money left because only a few months earlier he had spent most of his savings on constructing flats on our property.

Our problems were many and we discussed them quietly because we did not want Das to know about them. Radio Pakistan kept on repeating loudly Jinnah's assurance: 'You are free to go to your temples; you are free to go to your mosques ...' Every now and then, the programme was interrupted to announce messages from some Hindus in India and Muslims in Pakistan inquiring about the whereabouts of their friends or relations. I heard one of my friends wanting to know where we were.

The entire atmosphere had changed into gloom. Sialkot was beginning to look different – and we were shut out from it. I wondered where Shafquat was and what he would be thinking. He was against the formation of Pakistan because like Maulana Azad, the Congress leader, Shafquat thought that Pakistan was a symbol of defeatism and had been built up on the analogy of the Jewish demand for a national home. He would often tell me that it was a confession that Indian Muslims could not hold their own in India as a whole and would be content to withdraw to a corner specially reserved for them.

It was dark when we stirred out of the room where we had stayed huddled the whole day. Sialkot's skyline was aglow. Fires were burning and the houses were silhouetted against the sky. We were watching the ghastly scene, when my mother tiptoed to me and tapped my shoulder to whisper: 'These are not fires. They are lights to celebrate your birthday.' I suddenly remembered it was 14 August, my birthday. Pakistan was born the same day.

A few days later, one rich Muslim family, my father's patients, tracked us down and insisted on our shifting to their vacant bungalow in the cantonment which was a relatively secure place. We accepted their generous gesture. Strange, the propaganda in Pakistan at that time was that the Hindus were *kafirs* (infidels). And here was a devout Muslim opening his house for us. Even otherwise, we had to leave Das's residence, as he was all set to go to India.

We collected our meagre belongings and drove to the huge bungalow in a big car my father's patient had sent. The drawing room was so large that five of us looked like a dot on a page. We were confused and did not know what to do next. We wanted to stay in Pakistan but did not like the trouble spreading in the name of religious identity. Rajinder would only repeat his remedy: there was no option except to migrate to India.

Word went around that the Doctor Sahib had taken up residence in a huge bungalow in the cantonment. Friends, relatives and acquaintances began to pour in. At one time, there were more than one hundred people under the same roof. The place soon became like a transit refugee camp. Most of our friends stayed until they could arrange their travel to India through Jammu, only twenty kilometres away. The authorities were of little help. I was surprised by the manner in which non-Muslims had been ousted from their houses and allowed the minimum of luggage. Some had been thrown out with the help of musclemen.

Still none had been physically attacked. The equation between the two communities had saved Sialkot. There were examples where people had bid tearful goodbyes to their neighbours. But somehow most of those who said goodbye believed that things would return to normalcy and they would be once again living together.

With this belief, we too decided to visit India for a short time till things settled down. We had no doubt that we would be coming back. But the odd man out, Rajinder, said that we would be lucky if all of us could reach India safely.

We thought that it was a communal riot which would subside after sometime. We had heard about riots in Bihar and elsewhere. Things always returned to normal. Since we had never seen a riot in Sialkot, our faith in each other's need to live together was greater.

Probably, it was our state of mind. But after some time the cantonment where we lived seemed to be back to the old days. One day, my mother and I hired a tonga to visit our house to collect clothes for the temporary visit to India. We did not know the driver. He was a Muslim. It was a distance of about ten kilometres but not even once did it occur to anybody in the family, not even Rajinder, that someone could attack us on the way. We could not imagine such a thing.

We found everything in the house intact. The Trunk Bazaar was as noisy as before. Many faces were unfamiliar but nobody gave us a second glance. Shafquat was there. I had sent him a message.

I offered him my library till our return. He refused to accept it, saying that the Muslim League would hound him if he were to remove even a single book. Nawab, a colleague on the peace committee, was different. He lived in poor conditions in a nearby village. He did not mind taking along with him a table fan and an iron.

When we had hurriedly left home on 14 August, my mother

had carried with her a precious *shahtoosh* shawl. Today she carefully folded it and put it back in her trunk, taking with her an ordinary Kulu shawl. She said she did not want to spoil her good shawl by taking it to India. I had taken with me the hardcover, *Jean Christopher* by Roman Rolland. I put it back on the shelf and picked up a soft cover, *Poverty and People,* which I thought I could afford to throw away in India before returning to Pakistan. My mother packed two suitcases, one for me and my two brothers and the other for my father and herself.

Shafquat and Nawab left us alone. We sat for some time at the same dining table from which we had accompanied Das to his house in the jail. My mother and I were sad in our own way. We were probably pushing back the thought that we might not come back, not to mention the feeling that we had lost everything and would have to start our life from scratch in India. Neither of us realized that it was the last visit to our house but something within us told us that it was goodbye.

I wish I could have words to describe the poignancy of those moments. But then nobody has painted the way the sun sets. Even Van Gogh couldn't. How could I describe the pangs of leaving everything behind? It was like crushing beneath one's shoes the embers of memory. It was a fear that everything had been reduced to ashes. It was all over.

Both of us hurriedly paid obeisance to Pir Sahib. We were taking leave from our elder who had looked after our welfare for decades. The grave had accumulated a lot of dry leaves and dust. We let it remain, thinking that it would be the same even after we had cleaned it. No one would look after it.

How strange that some months earlier a group of Muslims had forced us to give a right of way to the grave through our property.

They had insisted that it was their right to offer prayers at every *mazar*. We did not want a legal battle on our hands and constructed a covered passage to the grave. A few Muslims came after that for about a week and then none.

We re-locked the house. While doing so, my mother remarked that if anyone wanted to break in, the lock would not deter them from doing so.

Our return journey to the cantonment was in the same tonga, which was waiting for us. We were now becoming excited because we were going to India. Setting aside the dilemma of what to do immediately, we were confident that this visit would help us take a final decision.

A few days before our return to our home, three persons came one afternoon to my father to take him to their house, where one of their sons was lying dangerously ill. My mother was not in favour of the visit. But my father prevailed upon her with the argument that they were his old patients whom he could not refuse. Clad in his *khaddar* kurta and pyjama with the round black cap, my father looked so desolate and so disturbed in the tonga. But I saw a still more shattered face on his return. My father wanted to be left alone. After some time, he told us that on his return journey, one Muslim boy, Bashir, whom he recognized, had thrown a brick at him. It didn't hit him physically but it had disturbed him mentally. He went on asking himself why Bashir had done such a thing when he had healed him of typhoid only a few weeks earlier. We were so shocked that no one uttered a word. Somehow, Rajinder's face told me that he had warned us against such happenings.

The following morning I heard someone crying and seeking my father's forgiveness. I found it was Bashir, whose father and uncle had brought him to offer apologies. My father was moved and he embraced the boy. When they left, we seriously wondered whether we could live in Sialkot any more, though we decided to defer a decision until after our visit to India. One month had passed by after Partition.

THE JOURNEY TO INDIA

On 12 September, when we were discussing our travel plans, a Hindu army major, on transfer to India, came to bid goodbye to my father. He was indebted to him for the medical attention my father had given to his children. The major inquired if he could do anything for him. 'Take my three sons with you', pat came my father's reply. The major was obviously embarrassed. He said he wished he could but there was no space in his jeep. However, after talking to his wife, who was sitting in the jeep, he said they could probably accommodate one. My father thanked him. He said his jeep would come the next morning.

After he left, we began discussing who should go first. All three of us implored one another to go. We could reach no agreement. My mother was listening to our wrangling all the time. Then, in the midst of discussions, my younger brother described how Nawab had come in my absence to tell them to send me away because some people had expressed anger over my peace efforts. Now there was no discussion. The entire family insisted on my accompanying the major. But when they found me unrelenting, my father suggested we draw lots. Whether it was managed or accidental, I was the unwilling winner. I tried my best to wriggle out of the situation but everyone said that Providence had made the decision. I did not sleep that night and after a long time I put my head in my mother's lap, asking her to caress my hair as she used to when I was only a few years old. I wanted to go back to the days when I had no worry, no fear. I was afraid now and wanted to cling to each one of them as if we might not meet again. There were numerous stories of migrants being killed on their way to Pakistan or India. Many trains had all non-Muslim passengers killed in Pakistan and Muslims in India. I imagined the worst and slipped into sleep.

The next morning, on 13 September, the major's jeep arrived, crammed with luggage and his two children. There was also a gunman sitting at the back. My mother had packed two trousers and two shirts in a handbag she handed over to me. She also gave me Rs 150. While weeping, she reminded me to stay at Daryaganj, Delhi, with her sister, Kunto Masi, who was married to a head clerk at the Central Secretariat. I had stayed with them once before when all was well.

The parting was short and quick. The major was in a hurry. I still had not reconciled myself to the prospect of leaving without being sure that my parents and the two brothers would cross the border in the next few days. They promised to travel to Narowal junction, about forty kilometres away, where a railway bridge provided a crossing to India. Those going to India had to cross the bridge on foot.

We promised not to say goodbye but our eyes were moist. We undertook to meet at Delhi at Kunto Masi's place on 10 October, nearly a month later. My last advice to them was not to travel together. We should not lose the family at one go. We knew that migrants were being attacked on the way.

As I got into the jeep, I looked towards my mother who was trying to hold back her tears. My father was stunned and distraught. He and my mother felt relieved, however, that at least one family member would be making it to safety. My brothers were laughing but how unreal their laughter was!

It was too early for regular traffic. The road was practically empty. Sialkot was not a large city. We reached the outskirts in a few minutes. A tall church separated the city from the countryside. We had to cover about fifteen kilometres to reach the Grand Trunk Road, which went all the way to Lahore and Amritsar, the border.

I had never imagined that the road would be so choked with people. It looked as if the whole of humanity was on the move. Our jeep was in the midst of a sea of humanity, inundating every inch of space – the road, the fields and the elevated rail-track. All streams except one were flowing towards India. That one was of Muslims coming from India with skimpy belongings on their heads. Hindus and Sikhs going towards India too had very little luggage. People rushed towards us. The jeep came to a halt. Some determined men and women stood on the road. They wanted us to hear them.

The scene was tragic. It was an avalanche of migration. Lakhs of people were on the move on both sides. None had expected to leave home. None wanted it. But none could help it. The two countries blamed each other as they tried to grapple with this and other chaotic problems within hours of the heady atmosphere of Independence.

An old Sikh, with a flowing beard flecked with grey, nudged me and tried to hand over his grandson. 'He is all we have in the family,' he begged. 'Take him to India. At least he should live.' A middle-aged woman tried to put her child in the jeep. 'I will trace you and collect my son', she said. But how could I take their children with me?

Every human being has limits to how much he or she can take of grief or joy, good or bad. I reached the level where I could take no more. My feelings had been dulled. It was as if I was left with no emotions to react. A story of brutal murder or gang rape did not move me any more. I just listened to gruesome happenings as if going through an exercise. Any narration, however touching, was like a narration I had heard before. The cruelty was the common factor. But at least some of them had got their stories off their chests. They probably felt better and withdrew to make room for the jeep to pass.

It was still a long way to the border. The major did not want to lose the daylight. The jeep sputtered into motion. I looked back. I could see outstretched hands asking for help.

The spectacle jolted me out of my wishful thinking that things would normalize and permit us to go back. I realized there was no going back. It would be a new life which I would have to build in India from scratch. I wished I could tell this to my father, who at the age of sixty-five would have to start all over again. His lifetime earnings were all in Sialkot – the property, his medical practice and everything. We were paupers.

Strange, no leader had prepared us for this eventuality. Soon after Partition, their speeches talked about the tragedy but gave us the impression that there would be no wholesale change. Only now did I realize that a sheltered upper middle-class life had lulled us into unreality. This was the biggest migration of people in history but no one had anticipated it. Hindus and Sikhs from Punjab were crossing over to the Indian side and Muslims to Pakistan. The ethnic cleansing in Punjab was almost total.

As the jeep drove along the Grand Trunk Road, I saw dead bodies on both sides, the smouldering remains of burnt vehicles and pieces of luggage strewn all over. More hideous was the sight of children impaled on swords or spears and women and men cut to pieces. They bore testimony to the hell that the people on both sides had gone through. And all in the name of religion which was supposed to represent values.

We had killed one million of one another and uprooted twenty million. Temples, mosques and gurudwaras had been demolished in hundreds. The subcontinent's composite culture and pluralistic society going back hundreds of years lay in tatters.

It was late in the afternoon when the jeep reached the outskirts of Lahore. It halted there. We were told that a caravan of Muslims had been attacked at Amritsar and that the Muslims in Lahore were waiting on the roadside to take revenge. We got down and waited in fear and silence. There was some stray shooting in the distance. The stench of decomposed flesh from nearby fields hung in the air. We could hear people shouting slogans: *Allah Ho Akbar, Ya Ali* and *Pakistan Zindabad.* But it was far away. We set off again.

There was nervousness as we approached the border. And then we heard *Bharat Mata Ki Jai.* We drove past the hurriedly erected whitewashed drums and the Indian flag on a bamboo pole that marked the border. There was rejoicing and people on the Indian side hugged one another.

It was great to be alive. There was still daylight. As I looked out, relieved and happy, I saw people walking in the opposite direction. They were Muslims. I saw the same pain etched on their faces. They trudged along with their belongings bundled on their heads and their frightened children trailing behind. They too had left behind their home and hearth, friends and hopes. They too had been broken on the wrack of history. A caravan from our side was going to Pakistan. We stopped to make way for them. They too stopped. But no one spoke. We looked at one another with sympathy, not fear. A strange understanding cropped up between us. It was a spontaneous kinship, of hurt, loss and helplessness. Both were refugees.

The railway platform at Amritsar was so crowded that it was difficult to move without requesting someone to make way. People obliged quickly. Had the tragedy made them humane or had it

taught them humility? It was so noisy that I had to shout at the top
of my voice to make myself heard.

I did not know where they – hundreds of them – were going.
Every train which arrived would be full in no time. I waited for the
Frontier Mail to go to Delhi. I had to use all my force to get in.
Squeezing in the bag required even greater strength.

I was taken for a Muslim in the second class compartment
in which I travelled. Non-Sikh Punjabis on both sides looked alike.
They dressed in the same way. They ate the same food and even
behaved in the same way. Everyone was condemning their leaders
for letting them down. But I was abusing them at the top of my
voice. I got attention, no doubt, but also some hostile looks.

My bare right arm flashed the crescent and star which I had got
tattooed at Sialkot. I heard whispers of suspicion about my identity.
Was he a Muslim abusing loudly to cover up his religion? The tattoo
heightened the suspicion and convinced more and more people that
I was Muslim.

I was pulled out of the compartment at Ludhiana, coincidentally
the city where most people from Sialkot had migrated. Burly Sikhs
with spears and swords joined a hostile crowd around me at the
platform, asking me to prove that I was a Hindu. I could see blood
in their eyes. Before I could pull my pants down, a *halwai* (sweet-
meat seller) from Sialkot, from our locality itself, came to my rescue.
He shouted that I was Doctor Sahib's son. Another joined him to
confirm and the unbelieving people dispersed. This ended my agony
as well as the excitement of the spectators. I was let off. But those few
minutes still haunt me. There was no mercy those days.

ARRIVING IN DELHI

Our train was diverted. It took one day more to reach Delhi, which was in the throes of riots. I went straight to Daryaganj where my Kunto Masi lived. Muslims were fleeing the city, leaving their homes and hearths behind, as we had done. It was a replay of the same sordid drama; only the victims had changed.

Connaught Circus, at the heart of Lutyens' New Delhi, was a shopping centre like the Mall at Lahore. The Mall had only one Muslim shop. But at Connaught Circus, there were quite a few Muslim shops selling mostly leather goods, particularly shoes. Here and elsewhere, the Muslim-owned shops were looted in the presence of policemen, the same pattern as in Pakistan. Here too the state had issued instructions to the police to deal with the looters firmly. Subsequently, orders to shoot were also issued. But when the force itself had got contaminated it was difficult to see non-partisanship.

Prime Minister Jawaharlal Nehru was so irritated over the inaction of the authorities – there were photos in newspapers showing looters carrying off shoes and other goods in the presence of policemen – that he himself went after the looters at Connaught Place with a swagger-stick he generally carried when he went for a walk. The rioters were not mere looters. They were Hindu fanatics wanting to be level with their counterparts in Pakistan.

Muslim localities like Ballimaran and Daryaganj were tense but relatively safe. There was a large contingent of police posted outside. Every important crossing was littered with policemen. Yet the Muslim localities saw looters pillaging at will. Policemen were more worried about casualties than looting.

Red Fort, not too distant from these Muslim localities, became a big refugee camp. Primarily it was a transit point from where Muslims were carried in buses to Pakistan. There were also special trains for Muslims leaving India.

Despite the sweltering heat, many Muslims wore their *achkans*, a sartorial habit they had acquired over the years as part of their culture. Complaints of lost luggage were in hundreds. Most cases were genuine. Many Hindus forcibly took whatever luggage they could lay their hands on. The police too was a party to the looting. The looted were not too unhappy if their family was intact. They would count the heads all the time. Many believed that no privation was sufficient sacrifice to reach the promised land – Pakistan.

The onslaught of Partition visited the poor most. The Muslim elite in northern India had its contacts among the elite Hindus. Some Muslims stayed with Hindu and Sikh families till they could migrate to Pakistan. The public servants were in the best circumstances because they enjoyed all the facilities and their jobs were safe on the other side. Still, several thousand Muslim employees remained in India, the land of their forefathers, of Jama Masjid and Hazrat Nizamuddin.

The migration from Punjab on both sides was total. In Sindh too, the bulk of Hindus migrated, though thousands stayed back, some with small businesses and some under the protection of their Muslim landlords. The NWFP and Baluchistan saw very little killing. In these two provinces, both communities had unitedly fought against the demand for Pakistan. Over the years they had become warp and woof of the same society, which was one but recognized the identity of separate religions. Like Punjab, Delhi witnessed scenes of forcible eviction. But it was partial in Uttar Pradesh and Bihar.

The pattern was topsy-turvy. The Muslim elite, the educated and the otherwise adept in their profession left India, leaving behind the poor, uneducated and the small-scale artisans. They were helpless victims who supported the demand for Pakistan because it was a popular cause among the Muslims. None of them realized or understood that they would have to leave the land of their ancestors and to put down new roots in new environments. The Muslims who particularly bore the brunt were those in the north of India, where Hindus and Muslims had clashed economically and culturally. Hindus asked them to their face to leave India because 'they had their share' in the shape of Pakistan.

The Jama Masjid, in the heart of Old Delhi, was the area where I spent most of my time. It was close to Daryaganj where I lived and it was a place where the non-vegetarian food was cheap. Shouts of *Meerut key kabab* and *Lucknow ki biryani* from vendors with their hand-pulled carts attracted customers even during the middle of the day. These men were not worried about their future, unlike the inhabitants of Ballimaran or the Sadar Bazaar. They had decided to stay back in India but wondered whether they could. Threats of violence were fewer here but the sense of insecurity was more. They vainly looked for peace in the midst of devastation and deprivation. What could they do? They were resigned to their fate.

Parey rahin ya chaley jayen (should we stay put or should we go)? This was what the Muslims in this area discussed. How similar it was to the question we had asked ourselves in Sialkot. Many would ask me the same thing whenever I visited their localities or the refugee camps. I wondered if they were the same people who had shouted for years that they would rather die than give up the demand for a separate country. They were now a helpless lot.

The refugee camps reminded me of one I had visited in Sialkot city. How tragic the whole scene looked! I wondered where my parents and brothers would be. They might have gone to a refugee camp, I imagined. But then I was sure that they must be on their way to Delhi because we had fixed our meeting in Delhi.

Jinnah had tried to wean the Sikhs away from India on the promise of giving them an autonomous state (Azad Punjab) on the border of Pakistan but with Defence and Foreign Affairs under Karachi. Sikh leaders, Master Tara Singh, Baldev Singh and Gyani Kartar Singh, rejected the proposal. They suspected Pakistan's intentions. Master Tara Singh took his sword from its scabbard outside the Punjab Assembly and announced his determination to set up an independent Sikh state. But he and other Sikhs crossed into India like Hindu refugees.

At first, when the rioting began, Jinnah would not believe the stories of killing. Then he would stay glum. Subsequently, he attacked India for having conspired to finish Pakistan. He held the Sikhs responsible for polluting the atmosphere both in Pakistan and India.

His personal secretary, K.H. Khurshid, told me at Lahore that the Quaid-e-Azam had never visualized a large-scale migration or massacre. His idea of Pakistan, Khurshid said, was of a country which would follow a democratic system and which would span differences between Muslims and non-Muslims. It was a strange idea for someone who had long been talking of a 'pure' (Pak) Muslim country.

In India, when I reached Delhi, Sardar Patel was anxious that all Hindus and Sikhs should come out of West Pakistan. He cared little for the Muslims, who he thought had better leave since they had achieved what they wanted – Pakistan. This was in sharp contract to Jawaharlal Nehru's stand. He wanted Muslims to stay back and believed their safety as important as that of other Indians.

We, the refugees, carried with us to India not only bitterness and vengeful thoughts but also stories of atrocities at our birthplaces where we had lived peacefully with Muslims for centuries. Since Partition was on the basis of religious identity, the killings only furrowed hatred deep.

On paper, both India and Pakistan declared that 'there shall be no discrimination against those who before 15 August may have been political opponents.' In practice, there was neither accommodation nor forgiveness. The two countries behaved as the Congress Party and the Muslim League had done before Partition: running each other down and causing maximum damage in the process.

Whoever was to blame – or, rather, more to blame – the few weeks of madness on both sides of the border embittered relations between the two countries for the generations to come. They differed on every subject, at every step. Fear and mistrust of each other made even trivial matters major issues.

So bitter was the relationship at that time that I heard Jinnah was thinking of breaking off diplomatic relations with India. He genuinely believed that India wanted to destroy his country – a fear that torments Pakistan even today. He confided in Lord Ismay, chief of staff of Lord Mountbatten, who visited him at Karachi in September 1947, that 'there is no alternative but to fight it out'.

In fact, from the very day the two countries came into being recriminations began piling up. Pakistan particularly blamed India for not letting it establish itself. When the dislocation of train services owing to riots hampered the dispatch of government records from Delhi to Karachi, Pakistan saw in it an Indian plot to scuttle the new country's administration. (The delay helped Karachi because it was able to do away with red-tape for a few months!) And when the Joint Defence Council was disbanded four months earlier than scheduled (on 30 November 1947), the Pakistan government's conclusion was that it was a device to deprive it of military stores.

I was greatly disturbed because I wanted the two countries to settle down and talk about cooperation, not confrontation. New Delhi had not sent all the equipment and stores pledged at one time. Even Field Marshal Auchinleck, who continued in overall command of the armies of both Dominions, accused India of having designs to 'prevent Pakistan receiving her just share or indeed anything of arsenals and depots in India', and hailed Pakistan's attitude as 'reasonable and cooperative'.

What was most disconcerting at that time was the Kashmir war. The ruler, Maharaja Hari Singh had acceded to India. But Pakistan had not accepted this because it expected the Muslim-majority states to join the new Muslim country. India had intentionally not given Pakistan its share of arms at a time when its regular and irregular troops were advancing towards Kashmir's capital, Srinagar. Many people coming from Punjab would tell me that they saw trains and trains, full of Indian soldiers, going towards Jammu. I recalled my visits to that place nostalgically. It was only twenty kilometres from Sialkot and we, as students, would travel in a colourful tonga to have a picnic on the banks of the Tawi, a river flowing through the heart of Jammu.

Kashmir came in the way of New Delhi transferring to Karachi its share of the cash balances of undivided India. The Arbitration Tribunal had fixed Pakistan's share at Rs 75 crores. New Delhi paid only Rs 20 crores and withheld the rest because, to quote Sardar Patel, 'India cannot reasonably be asked to make payment of cash balances when an armed conflict with its (Pakistan's) forces is in progress.' Pakistan's reply was that at no stage of the negotiations was the Kashmir question 'ever mentioned or considered'; and, therefore, linking the two was an 'unfriendly act'.

An important section in the Indian government favoured the adjustment of Pakistan's share against the property we Hindus and Sikhs had left behind. A rough estimate was that evacuee property in Pakistan totalled Rs 500 crores ($375 million) as against Rs 100 crores ($75 million) in India – a ratio of five to one.

It was only after the protest fast by Mahatma Gandhi, who was appalled over the non-payment of dues to Karachi, that New Delhi did pay Pakistan's share. Patel never forgave the Mahatma for that. Nor did the extremist Hindus, one of whom assassinated him on 30 January 1948.

We, the Punjabis from the other side, were critical of him for not meeting his promise: 'Pakistan over my dead body.' Never did we imagine or want him to be killed. After his assassination we felt orphaned because he was not only a court of appeal for us but also a family head whom we could defy with confidence in his forgiveness and love. We cried the most. In our homes, food was not cooked the day he was cremated.

I wept and as I stood in the congregation at India Gate, as his cortege passed, I felt lonely. What would happen to Hindu-Muslim unity? I recalled his words at one of his prayer meetings I attended: 'You refugees are angry. But remember, Hindus and Muslims are my two eyes.'

The two countries fell out over trade as well. There was a standstill agreement to exempt from customs duty the goods shipped from India to Pakistan and vice-versa. It was a sort of Customs Union. But it was not working. Instead of rectifying the lapses, both countries began treating each other as 'foreign' for purposes of levying customs and excise duties. The result was that India looked to Egypt for cotton which could have been available from across the border and Pakistan hauled coal all the way from Great Britain and Australia instead of getting it from the mines next door in Bihar. When crossing the border a few months earlier I had imagined that the borders would be soft. After all, we were from the same stock.

Had there been any other bright patch in India-Pakistan relations, or had the peoples on both sides settled down to accept the reality of Partition, things might have been different. But the climate in the subcontinent was one of hate and hostilities, of revenge.

Across the border, an Indo-Pakistan Islamic League cropped up with the 'sole mission' to 'liberate' Muslims from the clutches of heartless Hindus. In India, the Jan Sangh, a successor to the Hindu Mahasabha, took up the cause of 're-uniting India'. The party would quote Patel's reported observation: 'Sooner than later, we shall again be united in common allegiance to our country.' Even Jinnah, who had promised that Pakistan would be a nation of both Muslims and Hindus, now faced pressure from the Muslim clergy or ulema who said that the concept of a secular state was not acceptable to them.

Indeed, Pakistan was a Muslim state, and however loud Nehru's assertions about secularism, Karachi considered India only a Hindu state. The Hindu-Muslim riots in the bazaars of the subcontinent before Partition became a Hindu-Muslim war across the border after it. The glory of the morning of Independence faded into dark conspiracies to destroy the other country. Soon it was twilight, presaging a long night.

One thing that came out clearly was that most of killings and looting were done by outsiders. Local people still protected members of the other community. So it was in Sialkot, even though there were a few casualties in our city. The cases of Muslims helping non-Muslims were many. Yet the general feeling in both the communities was that those with whom they and their forefathers had broken bread had turned their backs on them at their time of need.

Confused and overwhelmed by grief, one day I met Humayun Kabir, Maulana Azad's secretary. I wanted to check with him whether I could be a member of the delegation which Azad was to lead to Pakistan. He had printed an appeal in the press for volunteers and I had responded immediately in writing. The discussion with Kabir took a different turn. He said that the Muslims' demand for Pakistan was wrong. But the more the Hindus opposed it, the more the Muslims supported it as the most beneficial objective to achieve.

This was largely true. There was so much mistrust between the two countries that what was better for one was suspect for the other. It was the Hindu-Muslim divide which the British had cultivated and fostered for decades to perpetuate their rule. When the movement for Independence gained momentum, the Muslims were generally taken in by the propaganda that in a free India they would be at the mercy of the Hindus who would be in a preponderant majority. If they wanted to carve out an area where they could be in a majority, therefore, they had to have Pakistan, their own homeland.

A few, known as nationalist Muslims, warned against such an argument. Their plea was that a large number of Muslims would be left in India with the preponderant Hindu majority. Yet the demand for Pakistan was so deafening that their plea was not heard.

I had heard weightier reasoning from Azad when he addressed a public meeting at Lahore one and a half years before Partition. It was a big gathering and mainly of Muslims. I was still in the Law College. I went to hear him because I liked his Urdu and the manner in which he put across his point of view. He spoke against the creation of Pakistan and began his speech by explaining why he as a Muslim thought that Partition would hurt Muslims more than Hindus. If it could be shown that the scheme of Pakistan would benefit Muslims, he said he was prepared to accept it. But the truth was, as he saw it, that even if he were to examine the scheme from the point of view of the communal interests of Muslims, he was forced to conclude that it could in no way benefit them.

He said that India would be divided into two states: one with a majority of Muslims and the other of Hindus. The two states confronting one another offered no solution to the problems of one another's minorities and would lead to retribution and reprisals in either country. The Muslim minority within India, Azad said, would awaken overnight and discover that they had become aliens in the area where they had had their homelands for almost a thousand years. I saw people crying in agreement. That might have been the reason why Jinnah's Muslim League conquered Punjab the last, the province which is today the backbone of Pakistan.

MY EARLY DAYS IN JOURNALISM

The atmosphere at my aunt's place at Daryaganj was turning heavy. At one time I overheard her telling her husband that the refugees who had come from Pakistan would make them refugees in their own country. It was understandable. He was only a head clerk. That I must find a job quickly was my resolve from day one. But having a law degree I could not reconcile myself to the thought of joining the government as a clerk. 'Anything else but a clerk,' was my resolve.

I could not get an opening in any English newspapers but a Muslim-owned daily hired me because I was proficient in Urdu. *Anjam*, literally means the end, and I began my journalistic career from the end. I had to teach English and mathematics to the owner's two sons in addition to working the evening shift on the desk. The *Anjam* office was located in Ballimaran, a purely Muslim locality where a pall of tragedy hung in the atmosphere. The local people and their forefathers had lived in the labyrinth of lanes and by-lanes, with houses upon houses, with bamboo-shaded windows, the chiks, for generations. The narrowness of the locality gave the inhabitants, intimacy and security. They were talking to one another all the time. The womenfolk, generally in burqa, went down the lanes, even from house to house, but seldom beyond Ballimaran. The place reflected a culture of its own, Islamic no doubt, but humming with a catholicity that contact with other communities had fostered. Ghalib, the famous Urdu poet, had lived here nearly 150 years ago, expanding the horizon of the Ballimaran population. His unorthodox attitude had shielded Ballimaran's conservativeness but not its piety.

I was depressed by the spectacle because for me Partition was the assertion of odd aspects of religion: its frenzy and anger. The Muslims I met at Ballimaran and the adjoining Sadar Bazaar had fear writ large on their faces. They felt insecure and were rudderless. They wanted to turn over a new leaf in their lives and the Muslim press was their guide. But its *volte face* confused them. It began to run down the birth of Pakistan, which a few days earlier was the only solution to the problems of Muslims. Without giving readers any explanation, the Muslim press criticized even the concept of

Pakistan. The Hindus doing business in the area were relentless in their pressure on Muslims to migrate to Pakistan. They told them openly that they had no right to stay in India now that Pakistan had been created. This was exactly what Azad had told them would be the Hindus' argument.

The attitude of my Muslim colleagues towards me gave me a peep into the community's feelings. They treated me as if I was a number one citizen and they were number two. They behaved like a person with a hat in the hand. Their dependence on the generosity of the majority community was pathetic. They looked for crumbs, a kind word which would lift their spirits. Little did they realize that Pakistan was the cross which they, their children and grandchildren would have to bear for many, many years to come.

Muslims in India turned their attention to Azad whom they now saw as their saviour. Only a short time ago, they had abused him and had called him the Hindus' 'showboy'. Students of Aligarh Muslim University spat in his face when some days before Partition he travelled by rail through Aligarh on the way to Calcutta, his home town. Things had changed now and the Maulana became their refuge. In fact, most of them took no time to rally behind the nationalist Muslims who had fought for freedom along with Hindus.

COVERING GANDHI'S ASSASSINATION

As a cub reporter for *Anjam*, I covered the assassination of Mahatma Gandhi on 30 January 1948, over sixty years ago. On that day, I was watching the PTI ticker at my office when I saw a flash, 'Gandhi shot'. It was like losing a heartbeat. A colleague, who had a motorbike, dropped me at Birla House, where Gandhi stayed.

All through the journey from Ballimaran to what is now called Tees January Marg, I saw no extraordinary activity. As usual, Old

Delhi was congested with pedestrians and man-pulled rickshaws, while New Delhi was un-crowded. It was obvious that the news had not yet spread. However, the wooden gate at Birla House was closed. I did not like the look of the place. It wore an air of emptiness. Gandhi had died by the time I reached there. I showed my visiting card with the name of the paper printed on it. There was no hassle. I was not asked whether I was an accredited correspondent or not, probably because the person at the gate was not a policeman.

Not many people yet thronged the place. Some had lingered behind when the prayer was cancelled. Some were from an early stream which had begun to flow in after learning about the assassination. Then there was a flurry of activity among the few security men and Gandhi's intimate followers, swathed in white khadi, sitting at some distance, chanting mantras. I could spot Prime Minister Jawaharlal Nehru, Home Minister Sardar Patel and Defence Minister Baldev Singh. They looked distraught and distracted. In my presence, Governor-General Lord Mountbatten arrived and saluted the body of the Mahatma, by then raised high on a dais at the centre of the Birla House garden. 'Thank God, he was not a Punjabi,' Baldev Singh told Mountbatten. 'He was not a Muslim either and we are broadcasting this fact,' Baldev Singh added. This was a thoughtful act because the immediate inference was that a Muslim had killed the Mahatma.

By now the police was building up into a large force. Gandhi had never liked the fuss of security. Leaders should not shun the public, he would say. Although the men in khaki had taken over the place, none pushed me or any other person from the circle of spectators around the body.

After some time, I saw Nehru rushing towards the boundary

wall. All around Birla House there was a sea of humanity, singing Gandhi's favourite song: *Ishwar, Allah tere naam,* or shouting *Gandhi amar rahe* (long live Gandhi).

Nehru climbed onto the wall, while wiping his tears, and in a speech which foreshadowed his famous radio address to the nation, he told the crowd: 'The light has gone out of our lives and there is darkness everywhere … . The light has gone out, I said and yet I was wrong. For the light that shone in this country was no ordinary light: that light represented something more than the immediate present, it represented the living, the eternal truths, reminding us of the right path … .' Nehru broke down while speaking. So did the crowd. There was hardly a person without tears glistening on their cheeks. Emotion betrayed all of them.

I did not see Nathuram Godse, who had shot the Mahatma thrice from close range. Probably he had been locked in a room in Birla House itself or taken away by the police. But I saw a trickle of blood and some flowers strewn on the path which Gandhi had taken from the building to the place of prayer a couple of hours earlier. Even with scores of people around, the path looked desolate.

It may be the reflection of my own feelings but the atmosphere was heavy with the poignancy of sorrow. I could comprehend what the loss of Gandhi meant. I could see history exploding before my eyes. Perhaps I was too callow, only three months' old in journalism, or perhaps I had not yet been hardened by experience, despite the carnage of Partition I had witnessed. I wept unashamedly.

It was as if someone from the family had departed leaving his children lonely and orphaned. For me, it was also emotional pent-up purification, a catharsis of pent up anger which had swelled within me after knowing about the killings during the days of

Partition. Only a week earlier Gandhi had told B.C. Roy, the West Bengal chief minister: 'What's the good of my living? Neither the people nor those in power have any use of me. "Do or Die" becomes me more in the circumstances. I wish to die in harness, taking the name of God with my last breath.'

I strode to the prayer place and stood there for a long time. It had an air of asceticism and spiritualism about it. There was something which touched me from within. I remembered how only a few days earlier I was part of the audience at the Mahatma's meeting. That was the day when Madan Lal had exploded a bomb behind the shed where Gandhi sat to deliver his sermons. I had heard the noise but had not thought it anything more than the bursting of a cracker. Gandhi had shown little reaction to the explosion. He had continued with the prayer as if nothing had happened. I came to know only from the morning newspapers that it was a bomb.

I recalled the words he uttered at that time: Hindus and Muslims were his two eyes. Would the nation follow his voice which a fanatic Hindu had silenced? Would his mission for unity be completed after his sacrifice? At least, for the time being, I could see that the loss had fused the different religious communities, the Hindus, the Muslims, the Sikhs and the Christians into one multitude of sorrow. All constituted the nation in mourning.

There was an atmosphere of gloom in the newsroom when I returned to the office. I did not talk to anybody and looked at nothing at all. None disturbed me as I sank into the chair to write the story. I had a multitude of things to convey. I could not even hold my hands steady, nor put fingertips together. Some of the words I wrote were not legible because my tears had smudged them. The editor called me and asked me to tell him slowly what I had written. I broke down. It took me some time to gather myself and file the copy.

I was so overwhelmed by grief and anger that I did not translate an agency report which the editor had given me. It was about a communal riot which had broken out in Poona, the city from where Godse hailed. I was so upset that I did not want to hear mention of riots. Gandhi was a victim of Hindu-Muslim hatred. Why should I tell readers about communal riots? They had had enough of them. The paper missed the story.

The editor called me the following morning to his cabin, not to admonish me but to tell me that if I wanted to stay in journalism, I had to report whatever happened, whether good or bad, without letting my feelings cloud my judgement. I decided to stay in journalism. I have reported many communal riots since but every time I have wondered when Gandhi's words that Hindus and Muslims were his two eyes would come true. Would the different communities ever shed their bias? And when would we illuminate this land again with the fire he had instilled into us?

THE FAMILY RE-UNITED

Although *Anjam* was losing its circulation rapidly, it was still selling 70,000 copies daily. The biggest embarrassment that the paper faced was its advocacy of the two-nation theory. It had propagated the line that the Muslims and the Hindus because of their religion constituted two separate nations which had to part company. The paper was inundated with letters from its readers, abusing it for having created a hiatus between them and the Hindus through these writings.

Mohammad Sabri, the *Anjam*'s editor, would often say that the readers' anger was justified because the paper had disseminated the cult of separatism. He asked me one day to write an editorial – my first – to repudiate the two-nation theory. If the paper were to attack the thesis which it had presented, what effect would it have on the paper's credibility? In my edit, I twisted the meaning of the two-nation theory to argue that not only India but the entire world was divided into two nations: the haves and the have-nots. My argument did not mollify the readers. The circulation went on falling.

I was happy for other reasons: my family had joined me at Delhi as promised. But my parents had had a close brush with death. My two brothers were the first to leave Sialkot. They took the Narowal route, nearer to Amritsar. They were stranded for days at the refugee camp which had been set up on the other side of the railway bridge, connecting India and Pakistan. Only a few buses were plying between Narowal and Amritsar. The fare was exorbitant. But it was not only the fare which kept my brothers at the refugee camp; it was the whim of local officials. There was a long queue and the bribe worked. What ultimately helped my brothers was not the bribe but their education in medicine. Doctors were needed everywhere. They were readily carried to Amritsar once they disclosed that they were medical students.

My younger brother told me how he could not get out of his mind what he saw when he got down from the train at Narowal: in the twilight, women were being dragged from the train. Despite being brought up in secular traditions, he confessed that he was so mad at seeing this that he started thinking in terms of Hindu and Muslim. He said he realized that our eldest brother was right when he said that no non-Muslim would be allowed to stay in Pakistan. Both criticized me for believing in outmoded theories like secularism and pluralism.

He admitted later that the biggest mistake of his life was when he spurned a Muslim girl, seeking his help. At the refugee camp in Amritsar when he was giving an injection to some patient, a young Muslim woman came running to him for help. 'Doc, save me,' she implored. My brother said what came before his eyes at that moment was the scene at Narowal of women being dragged from the train. The man chasing the young woman stood at a distance for a while. But when my brother did not offer her protection, he dragged her to his side. My brother was in tears, which I believe was his catharsis.

My parents too had a hard time. My father's patients would not allow him to leave Sialkot. One day he and my mother reached the railway station without telling anyone and boarded a train to Narowal. But two young boys recognized them. Even on the assurance that they would return after a few days, the boys did not allow them to travel. Ultimately, they told them that all the persons on the train would be killed ten kilometres further on. They said that some of their friends had gone to the spot and were waiting for the train.

My parents had no choice except to leave the train and the boys took them back to the cantonment house. As foretold, all the passengers in the train were killed. The following day, the two boys brought my parents in a tonga from the house to the station and helped them board the train going to Narowal. The boys said they had made sure that no one would touch the train. None did.

My mother had a small suitcase of clothes and my father held lightly a small box containing jewellery and cash. When they were crossing the bridge at Narowal, some young man snatched the box from my father's hands and melted into the crowd.

They lost everything. When they reached Amritsar, they did not even have clothes to wear. Nakul Sen was then the deputy commissioner at Amritsar. He had served in Sialkot and had got close to the family. My parents rang him up. He gave my father his own clothes which did not fit. Nakul Sen was one foot shorter than my father.

Hearing their tale of troubles I wept. In fact, all of us wept. My brother Rajinder had turned out to be correct. We had had to leave Pakistan, the way he had predicted. But we felt relieved because we were all safe. My two brothers returned to their studies and I stayed with my parents who had transferred their money to a bank at Delhi. Our troubles were many but the fact that we had all reached Delhi made us happy.

MEETING HASRAT MOHANI AND SETTING OFF FOR THE USA

Anjam asked me to quit because of its economic difficulties. So I began work with *Wahadat,* which was published from a big hall in Ballimaran itself. The place was not far from *Anjam*. But *Wahadat* did not have the paraphernalia or prestige of a daily. The administration was housed somewhere else, to which I had no access. I was given the same monthly salary of Rs 100. Sometimes I suspected that the proprietor gave me the salary from his own pocket, knowing well that I was a refugee with no resources. Was this his penance for the Partition which he had supported?

Wahadat was an afternoon daily which required an early attendance. I could only manage to arrive by 8.30 am and sometimes even later because it took nearly an hour to cycle from Karol Bagh, the colony where most refugees had rented houses. Even otherwise, I was a late riser, a habit I had formed during my days at the Law College where the silence of the night provided a suitable environment for studies. Here, in Delhi, my mother woke me up to enable me to reach the office.

She broke down when I handed her my first pay in cash. *Anjam* had paid by cheque and I sent it straight to my savings account. She did not know my salary then. Her tears would not stop despite my consolation. She said she always thought that I would one day occupy a high position. But her dream was shattered when she found me cycling miles every day and getting a pittance. What was eating her up was my future.

This also bothered me at times. I could not imagine spending the rest of my life in an Urdu paper, or for that matter, in language journalism, because I was not good in Hindi. The same worry ate up another person whom I came to know at *Wahadat*. He would cough all the time in a corner of the hall where his bed rested on bricks. His coughing was a bit muted because all the time he would cover his body, including the mouth, with a quilt. No one complained about his coughing but I proposed one day to move his bed to some other place. Everyone on the news desk was horrified at this suggestion, as if I had committed a sacrilege.

I did not know who he was. All turned towards me and said that the person concerned was Hasrat Mohani. I had never met him but had followed his poetry and his sacrifices for the country's freedom. I had not liked his joining the Muslim League a few months before Partition. But that was the time when practically every Muslim had been swept off his feet with the prospect of an independent Muslim state. I respected Mohani immensely as a great Urdu poet but felt baffled over his decision to join the Muslim League. One day I went up to him and recited one couplet from his poetry:

Nahin ati to yad unki mahinon tak nahi ati
Magar jab yad ate hain to aksar yad ate hain.

(I may not remember her for months but when her memory catches up with me, I remember her often.)

He looked at me as if he was trying to place me. His face brightened when I told him I was a refugee who had come from Pakistan. He looked a tired man who had spent every ounce of energy for the cause of Independence. His former friend, Abul Kalam Azad, shunned him, and rightly so, because, for someone who had gone to jail under the leadership of Mahatma Gandhi, switching support to the demand for Pakistan, against which he had fought all his life, made no sense. Mohani was also a communist in his leanings.

'Our vision of Pakistan was different from what it has turned out to be,' Mohani said when I asked him why he joined the Muslim League. 'My idea was that of a secular country where the Muslims would be in a majority but within a pluralistic democratic system.' He was greatly shaken by the mass killings on both sides. But it was naïve not to expect them because there was an atmosphere of communal conflict before Partition.

Hasrat Mohani took a liking to me. He advised me to quit Urdu journalism which he said had no future in India. I resigned my job and went to America where I joined the Medill School of Journalism at Evanston near Chicago. A Fulbright grant enabled me to travel to New York. But I had very little money for boarding and lodging. Conditions at home had not yet improved to the extent that they could afford to pay for my studies.

I had to work my way through. I was a waiter at a boarding house and got two meals free. I worked on Saturday and Sunday, raking lawns, supervising an ice-skating rink at night and doing some odd jobs. One was to clean the windows of a skyscraper from the outside in Chicago in December.

At the beginning of my semester when I had no work, I would eat only a loaf of bread and take water throughout the day. I could not afford a hot meal. Even when I began earning I had a problem paying my fee. A part of it was waived but I had to put in extra effort to pay the rest. The problem arose when I had to submit my dissertation which had to be typed cleanly in triplicate. The Dean's secretary did the job in exchange for a sari I promised to send on return. I meant to do it but never did.

I had to leave Evanston two weeks before earning the M.Sc degree. I had applied for a job as an Information officer at the Ministry of External Affairs in Delhi. The Union Public Service Commission (UPSC) had fixed my interview in London. My sudden departure meant clearing my bills a fortnight earlier. I had to borrow two hundred dollars from Norman Cousins, editor of the *Saturday Review*, a prestigious weekly from New York. I had been his guide when he visited some refugee camps at Delhi.

Breaking my journey in London was of no avail. The UPSC rejected me. But the Medill School gave me the M.Sc degree in journalism, although I had left two weeks early. Sometimes I wonder whether I should have accepted a job I was offered at a provincial daily in America. But I wanted to return home early to contribute my bit to the family's depleted income. I resumed my journalism career, this time in English. India had launched its first five-year plan and I became a feature writer in the publicity department of the Planning Commission.

DELHI TRANSFORMED AND THE FATE OF THE OLD CULTURE

I had never lived in Delhi before migration. Many years earlier when I visited it for the first time to attend a friend's marriage I found it too classy for me. It gave me an uneasy feeling of being in a town of the upper crust where a middle-class person like me could not fit in. One posh business centre was Connaught Place which I found worth frequenting to see *mems* (white women). We, Indians and Pakistanis, have a strange fascination for them, not because they are connected with the Raj but because they are so different from our women in complexion, dress and deportment.

The colour 'white' is considered beautiful. Our literature is full of it, describing a beautiful woman as *mem*. Even in our day-to-day conversation, the highest compliment we pay to a woman is when we say she is like a *mem*. I remember when I was doing history honours at Forman Christian College at Lahore, our professor, Mr Vernapillai, from the South, would admonish us for colour bias. He was hurt because we would greet Mrs Wilson, a *mem*, not Mrs Vernapillai who was dark. We offered apologies to Mr Vernapillai but we still bowed when Mrs Wilson passed by in a straw hat. It was instinctive. I have not been able to figure out why even today we have not been able to overcome the bias. Was it because of one hundred and fifty years of slavery or because of our own colour prejudice? Women from Africa living in Delhi often complain about discrimination.

Connaught Place, an unending circular corridor, with a curved moulding above arched openings, at one time had many *mems*, but only a few remained after Partition. It was now thronged with us, the Punjabis, coming from the other side of the border. We brought our own culture with us. Women wore tight *salwar* and long *kameez*, the dress which Delhi and other northern cities copied subsequently. The *salwar* and *kameez* were associated with Muslims but they were part of Punjab's pluralistic culture. In fact, our oven-baked dishes, which we brought from Pakistan, were also to the liking of Delhiwallas. *Tandoori murgha, tandoori machli* and *tandoori paneer* became popular dishes in the entire north. The same recipes also travelled to the South, to the delight of Punjabis.

Yet, the informal behaviour and the back-slapping of Punjabis irritated the formal, slow-footed people of Delhi. They admired our forward-looking attitude but did not like our habit to dominate. We were too overbearing. Without realizing it, we crowded out the dainty, decent culture of Delhi with our crudeness and indiscipline.

Muslims living in different parts of Delhi slowly and gradually withdrew to the inner city. The fallout of Partition in terms of killings had also frightened them. Many Muslims migrated to Pakistan. It was a twist of fate that they had to take refuge at Red Fort, built by the Mughals, the Muslim kings.

What the migration harmed most was Urdu. This was the language which was spoken in and around Delhi and had roots in the area. This was a simple, folksy language which helped the common man to communicate. Since Urdu came to be adopted by Pakistan as its national language, it was considered 'foreign' in India to the disadvantage of millions who were familiar with it. The United Punjab had Urdu as its written language and Punjabi as the spoken one. This was as true of men as of women. I recall Maulana Azad saying that Urdu had lost its case with Partition. It came to be linked with Muslims. This was its undoing in India. The worst was that the teaching of Urdu was stopped in schools and colleges on our side of Punjab.

My mother and I corresponded in Urdu during my college days at Lahore. She knew Urdu but not a word of English. Both of us would often introduce Urdu verses in our writing. Even today,

Punjabis relish Urdu poetry. A substantial credit goes to them for having initiated a famous Urdu *Mushaira* at Delhi in 1948, one year after Partition. This continues even now. The wrong thing which we have done to Urdu is that we have Punjabized it because of our faulty pronunciation. Urdu lovers feel exasperated but they prefer to keep quiet because they know how much the Punjabis love Urdu and how honest they are in their efforts to revive it.

I have always been a strong advocate of Urdu, not only because it initiated me in journalism but also because I myself wrote Urdu poetry, which I gave up when Hasrat Mohani told me that I was wasting my time writing verses that made no sense. Yet Urdu is my first love and I have stuck to it faithfully. As a syndicated columnist, Urdu and Hindi are the only languages into which I translate my English piece each week.

Muslims in post-Independence India have made the neglect of Urdu one of their main grievances. They have a case. Urdu is listed as one of the national languages in the Constitution of India, yet it does not have its rightful place. The main reason is that when the states were reorganized after Independence on the basis of language, no state, except Jammu and Kashmir, adopted Urdu as its official language. In many states, even Muslims do not learn Urdu because it does not give them any advantage to get a job or pursue a career. I remember addressing the first All India Urdu Editors' Conference and telling them that Urdu had no future if it was not linked with employment.

Punjabis over the age of forty have stuck to Urdu because they feel at home with it. Subsequent generations have distanced themselves from the language and young Punjabis today are behaving in the same manner. The biggest disadvantage of this is that tomorrow, when the two Punjabs resolve their differences, there will be no handy Urdu language to cement the relationship. The gulf between Muslims and non-Muslims would have been easier to bridge if Urdu was still prevalent in Punjab. While the older generation remains emotionally attached to Urdu, the younger generation is unfamiliar with it. Yet, the older generation was bred in the spirit of give and take and they could be more generous in settling things than the younger one.

More than Urdu, it was the Delhi culture, fine and aesthetic that the Punjabis pulverized beyond recognition. In the city of Ghalib it became rare to hear chaste Urdu. This was perhaps inevitable because the Punjabis soon outnumbered the local population. Delhi was a small city before Partition, not even half a million people, whereas the number of migrants was somewhere near one million. Subsequently, the Punjabis themselves were reduced to a minority. Yet, Delhi was all Punjab in the fifties, the sixties and part of the seventies. In 1948, the then state chief minister even requested Prime Minister Jawaharlal Nehru, to give Old Delhi to Punjab for its capital. Haryana was then part of Punjab and Chandigarh was built long after. Nehru's reply aptly describes the Punjabis: 'You people want to grab everything.'

DELHI TODAY

When people from Pakistan visit Delhi today they find the city unrecognizable. At the time of Partition, Delhi was a city of distances. Qutab Minar was out in the wilderness and even Humayun's tomb, now in the heart of city, was far away. Both look so near today. I remember accompanying my father to Khan Market, where he was allotted a flat against our claim for the property left behind in Sialkot. This was in the early fifties. Both of us declined the rehabilitation ministry's offer. We felt that the place would never be rehabilitated. Today it is the most expensive property in India.

At that time, most of the Punjabi population was either in Old Delhi or in Karol Bagh, the localities where the Punjabis concentrate. Ajmal Khan Road, once part of Delhi's old culture, was converted into a Punjabi bazaar, with familiar smells and sounds. But we kept the names of localities as they were before Independence. We changed their profile but never called them Anarkali, Shalmi Gate or Mazang, the popular habitations which we had left behind at Lahore. By contrast, the migrants to Karachi, I found during my visit a few years ago, had named their habitations Banarsi *Chowk*, Aligarh *Muhalla* or Meerut *Abadi*, after the places they had left behind in Uttar Pradesh.

Ajmal Khan Road is today the most bustling market. Even the Punjabis from Pakistan make a beeline to the bazaar when they come for shopping for festivals or weddings. The most expensive clothes and jewellary are sold there. What attracts the Pakistanis is the atmosphere, which is just like the one back home.

They are also amazed how Delhi has expanded. Noida and Greater Noida in Uttar Pradesh at one end and Gurgaon and Manesar in Haryana at the other are the two points, 180 kilometres apart, between which Delhi pulsates and accommodates more than twelve million people. The city is still expanding and attracting more people and more investment. This expansion has told upon the environment. But it is not the fault of migrants. They too are victims of the haphazard growth and the government's policy to convert green spaces into a concrete jungle. The Ridge, older than the Himalayas, should be sacrosanct because it provides the city with its much-needed water. The builders' mafia, with the help of politicians and bureaucrats, is destroying not only the Ridge but other natural sources of water. A temple has been allowed to come up in the very bed of the Jamuna. More construction is planned there, despite the strong opposition of environmentalists. Law courts are of very little help because they are 'pro-development'. Those who protest against pollution or against destroying water resources are dubbed anti-progress.

On the other hand, more and more vehicles are on the road, polluting the atmosphere. A pall of smoke hangs over Delhi, making the city dirtier and darker day by day. I wonder what has happened to the green, broad Delhi to which I migrated in September 1947. I am not against development, nor the malls or the skyscrapers which have been coming up so quickly. But I am against destroying the soul of Delhi which is its flora and fauna.

Hundreds of years ago Delhi was deserted because it had no water. I do not want that to happen to the city again. I do not want to migrate again. Delhi is now my home as Sialkot was once. I have had my quota of sufferings in my lifetime. I have been broken on the wrack of history once. I do not want to be broken again by the mafia of builders, politicians and bureaucrats.

REVISITING SIALKOT

After Partition, Indian Punjab was reduced to one-third of its former size but the pull of the old province, the desire to go back to our roots, still remained strong. Probably, you never overcome the feelings which your place of birth evokes, just as in later life you recall the days of your youth. I always wanted to re-visit Sialkot city. But I could not do so because I could not get a visa. Since the city is adjacent to the Sialkot cantonment, the Pakistan intelligence agencies did not clear my name. However, when I was nominated to the Rajya Sabha, the upper house of the Indian Parliament, these obstacles were removed because legislators from the parliaments of SAARC countries were not required to get a visa.

When I re-visited Sialkot in 1972 I did not find it much changed. Youths still leaned against walls watching the world go by, just as my friends and I used to do for hours together in happier days long ago. There was the same squalor; the same unpainted houses huddled along narrow streets, now narrower because of shacks erected by the refugees who had come from the nearby Shakargarh district in the wake of hostilities between India and Pakistan. The school I had gone to had been transformed into Islamia Girls School. In my days there were only boys and co-education was not allowed. Another difference was that the spacious playing grounds had been devoured by new buildings put up to accommodate more students. Murray College, which I had attended, looked the same, with the oblong-shaped church in one corner. But the staff was new, except for an old peon, who was limping the way he did years ago. The nearby railway station, which was a recreation place for us, was in a shambles. Indian planes had destroyed it during hostilities. The debris remained un-disturbed and it was apparent that reconstruction was slow.

I wished, above all, to see my old home, but I was saving that to the last. When I saw it, I felt that nothing had changed: the same type of bamboo curtains, shielded the windows; the same cement projection with its flowerpots stood incongruously against the shabby surroundings. But it was a different house, somebody else's; a refugee from Delhi now occupied it. I thought of going in, but decided against it. Why should I disturb the privacy of the new owners?

I went to the back of the house to visit the Pir's grave. We used to adorn it every Thursday with flowers, and lighted a lamp.

Now the grave wore a forlorn look; weeds had grown all over it. I was told that nobody tended it any more because Islam did not permit idol worship. I did not agree to that. *Mazars* were not temples.

A part of the old fort, situated on a hillock opposite our house, had been destroyed in the 1965 war. A new road had been built to skirt the damaged portion. During the old days this fort was the highest point in the town, but now it was only a shaggy mound. Many tall buildings had come up. Below the fort lay a maze of streets. They were more crowded than I could recall. But nobody knew me. No one recognized me as I walked through bazaars.

The only person to stop me was an old man who asked if I was the son of Doctor Sahib. Even before I could answer him, he embraced me. Tears rolled down his cheeks. 'You used to call me "Chacha". Do you remember that?' he asked. I vaguely recognized him but he had changed considerably. Twenty-five years was a long gap and it was surprising that he could still remember me. By this time a crowd had gathered. Word had gone round that an Indian was in their midst. There was no hostility but much curiosity. People stood in small knots at a distance – just looking at me and talking among themselves. To me they were all strangers and I felt out of place. Suddenly it was a different town. Something had gone from the place – something never to return. A town is made not of bricks and mortar but of people and their neighbours. How could I find again the old familiar faces or the atmosphere I had inhaled for years? I did not want to stay any longer. I left the town in less than twenty-five minutes – the place for which I had waited for twenty-five years. Yet I recalled with sadness our decision to stay back in Sialkot after Partition.

RE-EXAMINING PARTITION

It was a strange Partition which left so many famous Muslim monuments on the Indian side and the sites of ancient Hindu civilizations on the Pakistan side. Even the line drawn to divide India and Pakistan had no real logic. In 1971, I went to see Lord Justice Cyril Radcliffe, the chairman of the Boundary Commission, to understand how he drew the line that divided the two countries. I met him in London when I was collecting material for my book, *Distant Neighbours: A Tale of the Subcontinent.*

Radcliffe had been a judge for a long time and it was probably his habit to wear a jacket whenever he met a visitor. But there was no formality in his manners. I found him a simple, straightforward person. He opened the door himself when I rang the bell of his flat. The room was cluttered with old furniture, with things he must have collected over the years. The living was austere. He had no servant, no maid, because he went himself to a kitchenette, which I could see from the sofa in the sitting room, to place a kettle on the burner to prepare tea.

'I had no doubt from the beginning that Lahore had to go to Pakistan and Calcutta to India,' Radcliffe told me. Lahore had Hindus and Sikhs in a slight majority over Muslims. The assets of non-Muslims were many times more than those of Muslims. But Radcliffe said he had no other option. 'I had to give them Lahore because they had to have a big city in West Punjab,' he added. He was defending the basis on which he had allotted Lahore to Pakistan.

This conversation took place in Radcliffe's flat in London on 5 October 1971. I was visiting Britain to meet Lord Mountbatten, the last British governor-general, and others involved in those fateful decisions.

After failing to get agreement that the UN should nominate the Boundary Commission's chairman, Muhammed Ali Jinnah, had suggested to Mountbatten the name of Sir Cyril Radcliffe, whom he had seen arguing intricate cases in the London courts. Jawaharlal Nehru had also approved his name after consulting 'that sneaky fellow Krishna Menon,' as Radcliffe put it during his talk with me.

There were two Boundary Commissions, one for West Pakistan and the other for East Pakistan. Each had four members. On the West Pakistan Commission, the four serving judges were: two from India, Mehar Chand Mahajan and Teja Singh, and two from Pakistan, Din Mohammed and Mohammed Munir. The East Pakistan Commission had C.C. Biswas and B.K. Mukherjee from West Bengal and Abu Saleh Mohammed and M. Akram from East Pakistan.

However, it was Radcliffe who ultimately made the decision on the boundaries between the two countries. The two boundary commissions appointed to support him were of little help because they were vertically divided – Indian members on one side and those from Pakistan on the other.

What yardstick did Radcliffe apply? I was keen to know. I found to my horror that beyond the broad objective to separate Muslim areas from non-Muslim ones, Radcliffe had no set of rules or guidelines to go by when he drew the boundaries. The task was such that no pre-conceived ideas were possible. He knew that he had to divide India on the basis of religion and that is what guided him. He had sufficient data by the time he came to demarcate the borders, since the commissions attached to him were exhaustive in their presentation. He had read tons of material as well. But he remained in Delhi; he did not visit any other part of the subcontinent.

The ticklish part of his assignment, he said, was to partition Punjab and Bengal where people spoke the same language but differed in faith. He appeared to have some kind of balance in mind. Therefore, his decision to give Lahore to Pakistan and Calcutta to India was understandable, although non-Muslim Punjabis did not appreciate the fact of Lahore going to Pakistan.

'Are you satisfied with the way you drew the border lines between India and Pakistan?' I asked. 'I was so rushed that I had no time to go into the details,' he replied. 'Even accurate district maps were not there and whatever material there was, was also inadequate. What could I have done in one and a half months?'

When I asked Radcliffe if he had any regrets, he said he had none, adding: 'I think I did injustice to non-Muslims in Punjab and Muslims in Bengal; both should have been given more territory than what they got.' Radcliffe said he never imagined that Kashmir, nor for that matter Gurdaspur or Ferozepur, would create any problem subsequently. He denied having had any talk on this matter with Mountbatten, who is alleged to have influenced Radcliffe to alter the dividing line in the northern part of Punjab so as to give India access to Kashmir.

Radcliffe was given very little time to finish his work. He also got delayed because, as a legal obligation, the provincial assemblies of Punjab and Bengal had to vote on the division of the two provinces. He told me: 'It was impossible to undertake a field survey because of the heat.' But Mountbatten, according to Maulana Azad, told Radcliffe that he could not delay the work even by a day. Mountbatten would telephone him at least twice a day.

Radcliffe was not happy with the members on the Boundary Commission. All that they did, he said, was to put across the point of view of the country they represented. Both sides wanted maximum territory and argued at cross-purposes. Once, a Muslim member from East Pakistan came to him in private and pleaded for Darjeeling's inclusion in Pakistan, saying 'My family goes to Darjeeling every summer and it would be hard on us if the place went to India.' Radcliffe had a good word for Mehar Chand Mahajan, the Indian Boundary Commission member, who subsequently became India's chief justice. He impressed Radcliffe with his erudition and legal knowledge.

'The Muslims in Pakistan nurture the grievance that you favoured India,' I told Radcliffe. He replied that they should be grateful to him because he had gone out of his way to give them Lahore 'which deserved to go to India. As it was, I favoured Muslims more than Hindus.'

It seemed that criticism of the boundaries he had delineated had reached his ears by the time I met him. He was irritated when I mentioned 'the unhappiness' of the Pakistanis. What hurt him most was the allegation that he had changed his report at Mountbatten's instance. The allegation of the Pakistanis was that Mountbatten had put pressure on Radcliffe to give India Gurdaspur to provide a link with Jammu and Kashmir. 'I was not even aware of the dispute over Kashmir,' Radcliffe said. 'I heard about it long after I returned to London.'

During the conversation, which lasted for more than an hour, I told him about the sharp differences between India and Pakistan over Kashmir. By that stage, he certainly was aware of them. He also knew about the wars the two countries had fought against each other. He felt sorry about what had happened. But he remained firm in his assertion that the only pressure exerted on him was to submit his report early.

Before saying goodbye to Radcliffe I posed the same question I had asked Mountbatten – 'Did Muhammed Ali Jinnah hesitate when Pakistan was conceded?' Mountbatten had said that he hadn't. Radcliffe's reply was: 'It is very unlikely.'

I also checked with him the veracity of Mountbatten's claim that he had warned Jinnah that 'his moth-eaten Pakistan would not last more than twenty-five years.' Radcliffe said, 'You are the first person to have told me this. I have never heard it before.'

It was ironical that Radcliffe, who divided India into two independent countries, advised 'some joint control' when it came to splitting the irrigation network of the Punjab between India and Pakistan. His award gave the irrigation canals to Pakistan and the rivers feeding them to India, while the controlling headworks were evenly divided. But he continued to hint at 'some joint control'. India's then prime minister, Jawaharlal Nehru, rejected it and characterized it as 'a political recommendation'.

Since there was no 'joint control', the two countries, after the division, argued endlessly over their respective rights. Pakistan said that the rivers were common to the subcontinent and maintained that it was the sole owner of the waters and the headworks in its territory. It became such a divisive issue that Pakistan suggested that the matter be referred to the International Court of Justice at the Hague. But Nehru opposed the idea on the ground that it would be 'a confession of our continued dependence on others'.

In 1951, when Pakistan was on the point of referring the dispute to the Security Council, an article by David E. Lilienthal, former chairman of the US Tennessee Valley Authority, appearing in an American magazine, saved the situation. He suggested a comprehensive engineering plan under which India and Pakistan could develop the entire Indus Basin jointly, 'perhaps with the help of the World Bank'. Apparently, Lilienthal had consulted Eugene E.

Block, the then World Bank chief, before writing the article. When India and Pakistan realized that America would give its blessings to the proposal and that funds were promised to make it happen, the development of the Indus Basin was found to be acceptable by both countries. But it took some time to bring the project to fruition.

In response to a formal proposal by the World Bank chief in November 1951, a 'working team' of engineers was appointed to tackle problems outside the political arena. India gave a guarantee not to disturb supplies until the end of the negotiations – and it kept its word, though Pakistan continued to make allegations to the contrary. For nine years, the negotiations between India and Pakistan took a long and tortuous route, and even in the last stages, both Nehru and Ayub Khan had to intervene to put the talks back on the track when the prejudice and cussedness of officials looked like derailing them. Pakistan had no problem because it was under military rule.

Nehru had to face criticism in Parliament for accepting 19 per cent of the Indus Basin waters and agreeing to continue deliveries till Pakistan built alternative channels. Indian engineers had prepared a formidable case to prove that both Punjab and Rajasthan would be practically ruined if India were to stay its hand for the ten-year transitional period. Morarji Desai, then a member of Nehru's cabinet, organized opposition from political quarters. Even Govind Ballabh Pant, the union home minister, who was loyal to Nehru, expressed his unhappiness over India's 'heavy contribution' to the Indus Basin Development Fund. He wanted to get it adjusted against the value of the property that Hindu refugees had left in Pakistan.

Nehru brushed aside all objections and the Indus Basin treaty was eventually signed in 1960 in Pakistan's capital, Karachi, by

Nehru and General Ayub Khan, then martial law administrator. Nehru was anxious to build good relations with Pakistan and thought a settlement of the water dispute would serve as the foundation upon which he could raise a durable structure of Indo-Pakistan amity. Why didn't it happen? Successive rulers at New Delhi and Islamabad should give the answer.

Nothing would be more futile than an argument now about who was responsible for the partition of the subcontinent. With the sequence of events stretching back for over six decades, such an exercise can only be an academic distraction. But it is clear that the differences between Hindus and Muslims had become so acute by the beginning of the forties that something like Partition had become inevitable.

For those who still regret the division, I can only say that the British could probably have kept the subcontinent united if they had been willing to ladle out more power in 1942 when Sir Stafford Cripps tried to reconcile the aspirations of the people of India with his limited brief. The congress party could also have done it if it had accepted in 1946 the Cabinet Mission's proposal for a Centre with limited powers, and zonal and provincial autonomy. But the 'ifs' of history are at best hypothetical and at worst subjective.

Has Partition served the purpose of the Muslims? I do not know. In Pakistan people avoid the word 'Partition'. On 14 August they celebrate their deliverance not so much from British rule as from the fear of Hindu rule. During my trips to that country, I have heard people say that they are happy that at least they have 'some place' where they feel secure, free of 'Hindu domination' or 'Hindu aggressiveness'. But I feel that the Muslims have been the biggest losers; they are now spread over three countries – India, Pakistan and Bangladesh. Imagine the influence that their numbers – their votes – could have commanded in the undivided subcontinent! They would have been more than one-third of the total population.

I do not see the subcontinent being reunited but I believe it is in the interest of the people on both sides of the border that the two states should live at peace with each other. Fifteen years ago, I began celebrating the independence of India and Pakistan on the night of 14-15 August by lighting candles at the Wagah border. I took some fifteen people from Delhi to begin the process. Now it is a peoples' movement. On the last occasion, there were 300,000 people at the border, including fifteen from Pakistan MPs with their families as well as some singers. The function starts at 8 pm on 14 August and ends at 12.30 am on 15 August because there is a half an hour difference in timing between the two countries. I started it because of the suspicion that the Muslims encountered whenever there were tense relations between India and Pakistan, which had an effect in both countries. From this year I have also started a campaign to speak Punjabi in our day-to-day life. Punjabis number 80 million in Pakistan and 20 million in India. I think their interaction will strengthen relations between the two countries.

By such means I hope that one day the high walls that fear and distrust have raised on the borders will crumble and the peoples of the subcontinent, without giving up their separate identities, will work together for the common good and share a common economic market. This might usher in an era fruitful beyond their dreams. This is the faith I have cherished ever since I left my home town, Sialkot, in Pakistan, over sixty years ago. And this is the straw I have clung to in the sea of hatred and hostility that has for long engulfed the subcontinent.

from bombay to karachi

asif noorani

For someone born in 1942, Independence and Partition remain a somewhat hazy memory. However, I distinctly remember being taken by my father to see the illuminations on some buildings. We enjoyed the view from the upper storey of a double-decker bus in Bombay. That was perhaps on the eve of Independence. I also recall the parade of the armed forces, a year later. The smartly turnedout soldiers passed through Pydhonie, not too far from where we lived.

My pre-Independence memory is restricted to raising the then popular slogan 'Up, up the national flag; down, down the Union Jack' with other boys, after school hours, for many days. The only Jack I knew in those days was the one who went up the hill with Jill, for that was my favourite nursery rhyme. I am sure most of the slogan-raisers from the missionary school, St Joseph's High School at Umerkhadi in Bombay were, like me, unaware of the meaning of the slogan and even the significance of Independence. When someone asked me why I was chanting the slogan, I said because all my friends were doing it too. I was at that time in what they called the Infant Class, the juniormost in the school.

I had earlier been to a kindergarten school called the
Dawoodbhoy Fazalbhoy School, which was run by the Ismailis
(followers of the Aga Khan). It was a good enough school but I
didn't like it for two reasons. For one thing, they served only
vegetarian food at lunchtime and, for another, all the kids were
made to take an afternoon nap. I was too restless to sleep at what
were odd hours to me. I simply couldn't close my eyes and was often
punished for not letting my 'neighbours' – the kids lying beside me
– go to sleep either. Eventually, a mattress was laid down for me in
one corner of the room so that I could not disturb my classmates.
My monthly reports said 'good' in all subjects and 'very good' in
English but 'bad' in the column for conduct.

Though the school was in a predominantly Muslim locality,
children from Hindu families were in significant numbers too. But
when the communal riots began, some Hindu children moved to
schools in what their parents thought were 'safer' environs.

St Joseph's School, where my parents had both studied, was in
what was considered a Hindu *muhalla,* but it had never seen any
riots, at least not while we were in Bombay – until September 1950.
Communal disturbances in those days were mostly confined to
areas such as Dadar, Parel, Kalbadevi, Gol Pitha, Madanpura and
Bhindi Bazaar.

My best friend in those days at St Joseph's was a boy called
Subhash Thorat. All I remember of him, apart from his name, is his
crew cut and a question that I asked him: 'Are you a Shia or a
Sunni?' To which he replied: 'I don't know. I'll ask my father.' I
somehow thought that Hindus could be Shias or Sunnis too. But I
wasn't sure who I was. I still wonder how the classification of the
two main Islamic sects entered my mind, for ours was a secular-
minded family of practicing Muslims. Sects, castes and communal

differences didn't matter to my elders, which is something I inherited from them.

The same question was asked four or five years later in Lahore after we migrated to Pakistan but this time I was at the receiving end. A girl from my class, with whom I shared my sweets, posed the same question. 'I guess I am a Sunni,' I said. 'Well, then I am a Shia. Remember! I can't marry a Sunni boy,' she responded with a grim face. I wasn't particularly interested in marrying her, at least not at the age of ten, but I did lament the loss of an option!

Back to Bombay – Our flat there was right in front of a mosque and one incident from the pre-Independence days, which is still quite clear in my memory, was the arrest of a man who was returning home after saying his early morning prayers, defying the curfew order. The sergeant who arrested him was British. My father, shouting from the third floor window, tried to plead his case, but this only annoyed the sergeant, who shouted back: 'Don't look out of the window or I'll have you arrested too.' My mother pulled my father in by his kurta and closed the window.

Shortly before Independence and for a few years after, communal riots became frequent in Bombay but they were never as bad as the carnage that shook the Punjab, Bihar and Bengal. Riots in those days erupted suddenly but were confined to a few localities. Cosmopolitan localities, such as Warden Road, Colaba, Napean Sea Road and suburbs like Bandra and Juhu, were free from the scourge. Curfew was imposed on affected areas immediately and peace returned after a week or so. Unlike in Gujarat, where the state government is widely believed to have sponsored the recent riots, the administration in Bombay during those days was non-partisan and keen on restoring normal conditions.

One day my father came home visibly shaken. As he stepped out of the medical store, of which he was a working partner, a group of Hindu fanatics on a truck had thrown a bottle of acid at him. He was lucky that the bottle landed a few feet away. Normally, that footpath outside Zakaria Masjid, built by my great grandfather, where the shop was located, had quite a few pedestrians but luckily at that time there was a gap, so no one was injured. Drops of acid did perforate my father's trousers but that was about all. In those days there was no traffic signal on the intersection of Masjid Bunder Road and Mohammed Ali Road and the traffic in the city was thin, which was why the fanatics could manage to escape from the scene.

Whenever riots broke out, my parents shifted, with me and my younger brother, to my maternal grandfather's flat in Dongri, which was bang opposite a graveyard reserved for the Ismaili community. The house was in a Muslim locality but only half a kilometre away the Hindus were in a majority. It was close to dusk and there were only a few minutes left for the curfew to commence. I saw a man in a white dhoti walking briskly to what would have been a safe haven for him, but he was intercepted by an Afghan, who jumped from the wall of the graveyard and stabbed the poor man in his chest. The man died then and there, while the assassin scaled the wall and disappeared. I had the misfortune of witnessing the murder from the balcony of my grandfather's second floor flat. For years the grim tragedy haunted my mind.

I have also not yet forgotten the hysterical screams of a woman in the neighbourhood whose younger son was murdered in a Hindu locality. He and his elder brother were returning home with their Christian friend after watching a movie at Opera House, when they were waylaid by a Hindu mob that wanted to settle scores with the

Muslims. The three boys declared themselves Christians and were allowed to go. The elder brother and his friend walked fast and the younger brother, feeling insecure, shouted '*Khuda ke wastey mujhe akela mat chodo.*' (For God's sake don't leave me behind). He was caught and clubbed to death, as the other two boys jumped into a moving bus.

But the defining moment in my thinking came when I was travelling in a bus. Communal riots had just ended but there was tension in the air. In those days eight passengers were allowed to stand on the lower deck of a double-decker. Like my parents I too was standing in the bus when a man in a dhoti offered to share his seat with me. My father told me to go and sit with the distinguished looking man but, out of fear, I refused to go to him. What was worse, I told my parents: 'This man is a Hindu, he will kill me.' The man smiled benignly and told me in a soft tone: 'Murderers are *mawalis* (the Bombay word for scoundrels). They are neither Hindus nor Muslims; they are simply murderers.' He seemed so disarming that I agreed to sit between him and his wife. My two fellow travellers asked me about my school and the games that I enjoyed playing. The lady stroked my cheeks and my hair. My perception of the Hindus changed.

This incident and the writings of progressive writers like Krishan Chander, Rajendra Singh Bedi, Khawaja Ahmad Abbas and Ismat Chughtai, which I read several years later, made my outlook completely secular.

Occasional riots in the city did not mar the excitement of my early years. I remember spending exciting vacations at Devlali and Lonawla, not to speak of Wadala, which was once a suburb of Bombay but is now a part of the crowded city. I distinctly remember one evening when I fell into a pond in Wadala but was rescued by a stranger, who had the presence of mind to hold me upside down so that the water inside my system could come out.

My favourite outing during those days, still fresh in my memory, was a trip to Victoria Garden, which was commonly called Rani Bagh. A life-size elephant, carved out of a huge rock outside the gate, attracted kids in no small measure. The fare inside was all the more exciting.

Our house opposite Ismail Habib Masjid in Chach Muhalla, close to Mohammed Ali Road, was in the midst of eateries. They served delicacies like *malpura, nankhatai, paye, qeemey wali roti* and all kinds of mouth-watering sweets and savouries. Our relatives from other parts of Bombay visited our *muhalla* to enjoy the gastronomical delights, particularly for *iftar*, the meal taken on completion of the fast during the holy month of Ramazan. Years later in 1976, Khushwant Singh, who was then the editor of the *Illustrated Weekly of India*, told me that every Ramazan he accompanied his assistant editor, Fatima Zakaria, to enjoy the Muslim cuisine.

For vegetarian meals, my parents used to take me to Prohit near Churchgate Station and to Vithal's outlet for *bhelpuri* close to New Empire Cinema. Vithal, the man who concocted *bhelpuri*, was quite old at that time. I don't know if the eatery is still there or not.

A restaurant opposite our house employed two people on shift to play records of film music. Each 78 rpm record ran for three minutes and the man in charge was responsible for hand-cranking the gramophone, changing needles and playing the flipside of the disc or taking out another record from its sleeve and replacing it. The session started around nine in the morning and continued till well after sunset. The breaks only came when the *muezzins* of the mosques in the vicinity climbed up the minarets and recited the *azaan* (the call for prayers) as loudly as they could. Later microphones were introduced and the *azaan* became audible even at greater distances.

I inherited my intense love for music from my mother and one of her brothers (who later, out of sheer admiration, named his son after composer Naushad). My mother used to sing merrily while doing her household chores. Songs from *Ratan, Shahjehan, Anmol Ghadi* and *Badi Behan* were among her favourites. And soon I started imitating her. Everyone who heard me sing *Jab dil hi toot gaya hum jee ke kya karenge* (When one's very heart is broken what's the point of going on living) could not help laughing. Imagine a seven-year-old-boy singing a song with such sad lyrics in a yet to be developed voice. Six years later in Karachi a lady in our neighbourhood once complained to my mother that at such a tender age I sang a shameless song – '*Hum to muhabbat karega duniya se nahee darega*' (I shall continue to love you and will not be deterred by taboos). She had found me singing the Kishore Kumar number while playing cricket and fielding near the boundary line. She felt that I should have restricted my talent to rendering children's ditties. But even this lady from Rampur (UP) didn't believe that music was *haram* (forbidden) in Islam, which sadly some fanatics in the NWFP think these days.

Every morning students of the Urdu medium school in the neighbourhood of my grandfather's house would sing in one voice the *milli tarana* written by Allama Iqbal: '*Sare jahan se achcha Hindustan hamara / Hum bulbulein hain uske, woh gulistan hamara.*' (Our Hindustan is the best in the world. We are its nightingales and to us it's a garden). Whoever composed the tune of the song did a really fine job. The tune was melodious and quick on the lips. Even today the poem by the national poet of Pakistan is held in high esteem in India. Towards the end of his life Iqbal dreamt of Partition and advocated the idea of a separate Muslim state in northwest India, though he never lived to see Pakistan come into being. He wrote another poem: *'Cheen-o-Arab hamara Hindustan hamara / Muslim hain hum watan hein sara jahan hamara.'* (China, Arabia and Hindustan are all ours / As Muslims the entire world is ours). But that poem was not chosen as the national anthem of Pakistan. Instead the poet Hafeez Jullundri was commissioned to write a fresh anthem and, strangely enough, its tune was composed by an Indian – a man called Chagla. Without being disrespectful to Tagore and Hafeez, one can say that the national anthems of both the countries – India and Pakistan – are beyond the understanding of the common man. One is highly Sanskritized and the other very Persianized.

While on languages, I may add that though my ancestors moved from Kutch to Bombay for greener pastures, even my great grandparents spoke Urdu and not Kutchi, which is a dialect of Sindhi. My mother was very particular that we spoke chaste Urdu instead of the Bombay-style Urdu, now quite popular in Hindi films. But ours was also a bilingual family. At school and among friends I spoke in English but at home it was Urdu all the way.

Sadly, Urdu has suffered at the hands of the fanatics on both sides of the Wagah border, who think that it is only the language of the Muslims. They forget that Hindus like Munshi Premchand and Firaq Gorakhpuri, from what is now known as the Hindi belt, and a host of Punjabi Hindu writers and poets have contributed to the richness of the language and its literature. Thanks to film lyricists like Sahir Ludhianvi, D.N. Madhok, Shakeel Badayuni, Rajendra Krishan, Majrooh Sultanpuri, Anand Bakhshi and Kaifi Azmi, and more recently Gulzar and Javed Akhtar, Urdu has continued to reach the masses. What we call Hindi film songs are almost always Urdu songs. One must admit that Hindi lyricists like Shailendra and Neeraj have written some memorable film songs too, though today, unfortunately, most film songs are inane and devoid of poetic sensibility. I can't help recalling the view of Mr I.K. Gujral, who, in an interview in 1997, told me: 'Unfortunately, those who thought that the Hindus and Muslims were one nation were also the ones who promoted Hindi at the cost of Urdu.'

The Bombay film world, like Hindustani classical music, has been enriched by members of both the major communities. Those who deny it are the Pakistanis who think that the history of the country started with the invasion of Sindh by Mohammed bin Qasim or their counterparts in India who bracket the Mughals with the British. They forget that while the former made India their home, the latter exploited the land they conquered and returned to their island after Independence; they never considered the subcontinent their home. Only the first and last Mughal rulers are buried outside the subcontinent: Babar in Kabul and Bahadur Shah Zafar in Rangoon (now Yangon) where he was taken against his wish after the uprising of 1857 and where he spent the last few years of his life.

Incidentally, one Mughal whose picture was displayed in some Irani restaurants of Bombay was Akbar, unarguably the greatest of all Mughals. The Irani restaurants in Bombay, like their counterparts in Karachi, had squarish marble table tops with antiquated chairs. The Iranis were either Bahai or Zoroastrians or Muslims but their cuisine was more or less the same. The Irani restaurant, which enjoyed the largest clientele in those days, was A-One Restaurant, located on Grant Road in Bombay. Its main attraction was the Parsi delicacy *dhansak*. I don't think I have ever had better *dhansak* than that served at A-One. But my favourite Irani restaurant was Café Royal in the Fort area of Bombay. My parents used to take me there after our visits to the Gateway of India. If I was lucky, I was also taken on a boat ride, but the treat was always a plate of chips, as French fries were called in those days. What they call chips these days were known as wafers in the Bombay of the late forties and early fifties.

The *bhelpuri* at Chowpatti was something I looked forward to eagerly. But compared to Chowpatti, Marine Drive, Juhu and Backbay were cleaner beaches. Outside St Joseph's School there was a man who sold *chana jor garam*, which, if I remember correctly, were roasted and spiced grams that were flattened to form a wafer. Father D'Souza, the school principal, wasn't too happy to see the vendor stormed by schoolboys at the first break, for he believed that it was unhygienic and bad for the bowels. The school hours were from nine in the morning to five in the evening, with two breaks in between. The longer one was the hour-long lunch break.

Father D'Souza loved to sermonize. He had speakers fixed in each classroom and sure enough every day he found a subject pertaining to morality. He invariably ended his five to ten minute discourses with one line: 'Money lost is little loss, time lost is a greater loss, but heaven lost is all loss.'

LEAVING BOMBAY

One incident, which is deeply etched on my memory, is the news of the assassination of Mahatma Gandhi. My parents were particularly worried about the safety of my uncle, Malik Noorani, and his wife, Mumtaz Noorani, both hardened leftists, who had gone to Delhi to attend the wedding of poet Ali Sardar Jafri and

Sultana at that time. Everyone feared that the assassin was a Muslim, so the marriage party was disrupted and all those present, including the newlyweds, fearing the outbreak of a communal riot, rushed to safer places. When it was confirmed that the assassin was a Hindu, policemen in trucks announced on their megaphones: '*Gandhiji ka qatal kisi Musulman ne naheen balke eik Hindu ne kiya hai.*' (Gandhiji was not assassinated by a Muslim, but by a Hindu). Thus, what could have led to as bloody a riot as the anti-Sikh riot in Delhi in 1984, after the two Sikh bodyguards of Indira Gandhi opened fire on her, was averted by the presence of mind shown by the authorities.

I remember clearly that one morning my father, who used to go out every day to pick up freshly baked bread and the day's copy of the *Times of India*, entered the house with a sullen face. He announced the death of Quaid-e-Azam, Muhammed Ali Jinnah. My knowledge of Mr Jinnah was confined to the slogans which some people in the neighbourhood used to raise: '*Quaid-e-Azam zindabad, Pakistan paindabad*'. But after Partition the slogans died down – discretion being the better part of valour.

Not all my elders were Muslim Leaguers. Some supported the Congress. But even those who were not in favour of Partition migrated to Pakistan in search of better opportunities. My father's brothers moved to Karachi first, while his father, half brothers and sisters didn't migrate until 1958. One sister is still in Bombay. As for my mother, her side of the family was determined to stay where they were, and they never regretted it.

Shortly after Partition, my father's friend, who was the major shareholder of the medical store run by my dad, shifted to Lahore. Normally, all those who migrated from India, except those from East Punjab, preferred Karachi because it was the capital of

Pakistan, but this man, commonly called Baba, chose Lahore because his best friend was from the capital of Punjab. He opened a medical store in Nila Gumbad, a locality in the heart of the city. It was so named because the mosque in the vicinity had a blue-coloured dome.

For a couple of years after Independence, the medical store in Bombay continued to do fairly good business. But one day my father received a notice from the Custodian of Evacuee Property saying that one Mr Popatlal, a refugee from Sindh, had been allotted the major share of the business in place of the man who had migrated to Pakistan.

Now things became difficult for my father. Even when Baba was in Bombay, he was not bothered about the business. He would come late, socialize with people and return home before sunset because he had trust in his partner. The kind of freedom my father enjoyed earlier was no more, for two reasons: Popatlal had no idea of running a medical store and he, understandably, did not trust the man who was running the show. Meanwhile, things became difficult in Lahore for Baba, who was too easy-going to run a business on his own. He just couldn't get up early, nor was he used to long working hours. Baba advised my father to come to Lahore and offered him the same position of a working partner, which he held in Bombay.

In 1950 my father, despite my mother's disagreement, decided to move to Pakistan. By that time free movement from India to Pakistan and vice versa had ended. The authorities on both sides had imposed what was known as a permit system. Passports and visas were to be introduced later. But before one could get the permit to move to Pakistan one had to get a no-objection certificate, which was a long process. There were many tense moments, both in struggling against the bureaucratic rigmarole and at the medical store, with Popatlal becoming more and more difficult. The tension began to show on my father, who was always lean and prone to sickness. Eventually, thanks to Mrs Fatima Ismail, a disciple of Mahatma Gandhi and a Congressite to the core, the no-objection certificate was obtained without further delay. My mother had by that time become reconciled to the idea of leaving India and her family for good.

THE JOURNEY TO PAKISTAN

On 3 September 1950 we left for the Princess Dock and boarded the Scindia Steamship Company's *S.S. Sabarmati*. My maternal grandfather, a widower, who had brought up four sons and two daughters after the death of his lovely wife, was shattered. My mother, the elder of his two daughters, was a pillar of strength to him, and here she was grief-stricken on board a ship, which was to take her, her husband and their kids to an unknown destination. In those days, film songs were played on the ship and before the ship steamed out of the harbour singer-actor Suraiya's popular ditty '*Ab hum na mil sakenge, tum hum ko bhool jao*' (You had better forget me for we cannot meet again ...) was played. Whoever chose the song did so at the wrong moment. As for me, the voyage was exciting. It was the end of a long struggle to get the elusive no-objection certificate and the permit to go to Pakistan.

The *S.S. Sabarmati* and its sister ship, the *S.S. Sarasvati*, took turns. Scindia Steamship operated a service between Bombay and Karachi every week. Every Saturday evening the ship would weigh anchor at the Princess Dock and drop it at Keamari, the natural port of Karachi on Monday morning. Except for the monsoon period – between early June and the end of September – the ship would stop in the open sea close to Mandvi, where a fresh batch of passengers would transfer from sailing boats and climb up ladders made of rope and wood – a rather uneasy exercise.

Since the monsoon season was in full swing, the small ship sailed straight to Karachi but there was a lot of rolling. The ship rolled and lurched endlessly from one side to the other. One could see the horizon swinging. It was next to impossible to hold a cup of tea without spilling its contents. A number of passengers suffered from nausea and some even vomited. My mother, already despondent, suffered no end, for she was prone to seasickness like many other passengers. I was the eldest of her three children – all sons – and I took care of my younger brothers as my father attended to our mother. We were in a second-class cabin, which was quite comfortable and a far cry from the crowded deck class.

It was quite an experience for someone whose longest journey by a boat was, till then, to the Elephanta Caves in Bombay. I could see the ocean all around and except for a brief glimpse of a coastline, there was no sign of land. 'What if the ship sank?' I asked the purser. 'Not to worry, we shall put you on one of these lifeboats,' he said smilingly, as he offered me a biscuit.

A solitary seagull at daybreak on Monday indicated that we were near our destination. Then there were two more seagulls, and just as I was looking for some more, I caught a glimpse of the lighthouse at Manora, an island a few miles away from Keamari, the harbour.

As the ship docked I saw something I had never seen before – a camel cart. Until then I had seen camels only at the zoo or at Juhu beach for young and old to take a joyride. In Karachi the poor ship of the desert was made to pull a large cart. As if that was not enough, I saw donkey carts too. In Bombay I had just seen bullock carts. Later I learnt that even in Rajasthan there were camel and donkey carts.

Karachi's broad roads were a welcome sight, but its grimy single carriage trams, run on diesel instead of electricity, unlike trams elsewhere in the subcontinent, were a disappointment. Incidentally, Bombay was the only city apart from Hong Kong in Asia to have double-decker trams.

Burnes Road, where we stayed with one of my uncles and his family, was reminiscent of Dongri and the *muhallas* around it. There were small flats, most of which were once owned by Hindus, who had left for India. Karachi had seen no riots except the one that was sparked by some refugees from India, who had lost their property and wanted to grab the houses and business of the Hindus.

We stayed in Karachi for two months, while my father went to Lahore to look for accommodation. He came with the bad news that Baba had gone back on his word and had offered to take on my father as an employee and not as a working partner. We had no choice. But Baba's wife, a distant cousin of my father, came to the family's rescue. She said that until we found a house of our own she would gladly offer us two rooms in the large bungalow that they had been allotted in lieu of the apartment and some other property they had left behind in Bombay.

TRAVELLING TO LAHORE

We left for Lahore on 4 November 1950. The journey by Pakistan Express (later renamed Karachi Express) wasn't too comfortable, for sand flew into the compartment, despite closing the windows and the door. It hurt our faces and eyes alike. It was no patch on the rail journey from Bombay to Poona or Devlali, where one saw lush greenery on both sides of the track; a large part of the trip to Lahore was through the desert. But as we entered central Punjab the landscape changed: there were fields all over. Today if you take that trip you will find that even in Sindh, thanks to the irrigation system, the desert has been converted into green fields. Also the express trains are now usually air-conditioned, so the problem of dust and sand is no more.

Model Town, where we lived in Lahore, was a lovely suburb. It was built, mainly by the Sikhs and the Hindus, in the late twenties and early thirties. Seven miles away from the main city, it was in those days the ultimate in town planning. The plan was completely geometrical. It had a circular road in the middle. There was a club, a hospital, a large mosque, a gurudwara and a mandir. The latter two, like the mosques in East Punjab, became residences for refugees after Partition when there was cross-migration of population on a stupendous scale.

The *kothis*, as the large bungalows were called, had sprawling lawns and tall trees. The one fruit tree that was common to all gardens was the jamun tree. The covered area of the bungalows was invariably less than half. Originally these grand houses were built by retired government officers, doctors and engineers. It was a calm and quiet place to spend one's twilight years. The Model Town Cooperative Housing Society faced a big problem after Partition when the Hindu and Sikh committee members left for India. It was reminiscent of the situation in the Fine Arts Department of the Punjab University where, according to Salima Hashmi, artist and art critic, there were 200 female students when the university closed for summer holidays in 1947, but when it opened after Partition in September, only five students – all Muslims – were left.

One could see a lot of Hindu and Sikh owners' names, along with the names of the houses, engraved on marble plaques embedded into the gateposts. On my last visit to Lahore a couple of years ago I was pleasantly surprised to find some names still there.

Tahir Mirza, the late editor of Pakistan's leading daily *Dawn*, who started his career with Lucknow's *Pioneer*, used to live in a bungalow called Ishwar Niwas, and according to his son, the marble nameplate is still there. The bungalow was once owned by a man called Ishwar Das Khanna.

Baba and his family had reached Model Town, where his friend Abdur Rahman and his parents lived, in September 1947. They stayed in a bungalow whose occupants had left only a day or two earlier. 'The food was laid out and the bottles of pickles were uncapped,' recalls Farida Gaya, who was barely ten when the family migrated. By the time they were allotted *Peace Haven*, every movable item had been stolen. Only some idols of gods were left because they served no one's purpose. Farida's mother, a noble soul, put them in a box safely. Years later when the original owners of the bungalow came to Lahore to see their house, they were overjoyed to see the idols which were from the days of their forefathers. Needless to say, they took them back to India.

The stories narrated by those who crossed the border into Pakistan were quite similar too. We met a family whose child was mentally challenged. When their village near Amritsar was attacked by a group of Sikh fanatics, they decided to lock their house and return when the riots subsided. On their way to Pakistan they passed through a village, which had till then remained peaceful, so they left the child in the care of friends, who lived there. A couple of days later that village was also attacked. The people who were supposed to take care of the child ran for their lives and in sheer haste forgot to take the child along. They joined a caravan of Muslims escaping to Pakistan. All the people in the caravan were killed, and that included men, women and children. But the child they had left behind was lucky. She was discovered by a Sikh tonga walla, who dropped her at Amritsar railway station, where she boarded a train that reached Pakistan safely. A few days later the girl was spotted by her parents in a refugee camp.

Abdur Rahman, who died a couple of years ago when he was in his eighties, recalled that until the Radcliffe Award was announced, just after Partition, no one was sure if Lahore would be a part of India or would be allotted to Pakistan. At one time there were strong rumours that Lahore would be partitioned too. One side of the canal that bifurcated Lahore would go to India and the other part to Pakistan. Rahman and his best friend Chhabra, who later settled down in Lucknow, decided that at an agreed time every morning they would stand at a particular point on the two sides of the canal and talk to each other. 'Not to worry. This will be a short-term arrangement because the country is bound to unite once again,' said Chhabra, a remark that didn't go down well with his Muslim friend. The last time they met was when Rahman's family members invited Chhabra to visit him a couple of days before his eighty-first birthday. The two friends stayed together in Model Town and drifted down memory lane.

Model Town, more than other parts of Lahore, was open and green. There were fields and orchards all over. A lot of bungalows had buffaloes in their backyards, which met the milk requirements of the owners and even their servants. The refugees, including us, had no such precious possessions. We had to rely on the milk that the farmers sold. Since I was the eldest son, it was my duty to walk early in the morning to the nearest farm, with a small pail in my hand, to get milk that was freshly squeezed from the buffalo's udders in my presence. During winters my mother made sure that I was covered with layers of woollen clothes and that my head and a part of my face were covered with a woollen muffler. What bothered me more than the intense cold was the farmer's dog, whose bark was supposed to be worse than his bite. But he reconciled himself to my intrusion into his inner sanctum well before I got used to going out to get milk early in the morning. In Bombay, bottles of pasteurized milk were delivered to our doorstep. A bigger ordeal was the non-availability of cooking gas in cylinders, which were so common in Bombay. Even charcoal was hard to get in Lahore. My poor mother had a hard time lighting fires, more so during the rainy season, when the wood was damp. She had to blow through a cylindrical tube to help the wood to burn until it was well lit. But one exciting thing, which we saw in Model Town and nowhere else, were glow-worms. Sadly, today they are no more.

One enjoyed taking long walks, particularly in spring and autumn. Motorized vehicles were very few. People either walked or pedalled their way to the market or their schools or colleges. It was not unusual to see teenage girls and young women riding bicycles. The sight reminded my mother of *Khazanchi*, a Lahore movie of the early forties, where a bevy of beautiful girls where shown 'singing' the chorus *'Sawan ke nazarey hain'*, as they exercised their pedal power.

Sitting in gentle sunlight during winters was quite a pleasant pastime, more so if one had a plate of pine nuts to feast on. At Model Town's New School, where I studied during the two-and-a-half years we spent in Lahore before moving to Karachi, desks and chairs were brought out on the sprawling lawns of the school in December and January. Sometimes the octogenarian principal, Miss Stratford, an English woman who refused to go back home, also moved her office to one corner of the lawn. It was like her compatriots of the Raj period shifting their capital to Shimla from Delhi during summers. Miss Stratford didn't speak Urdu or Punjabi at all, but when teaching the difference between proper noun and common noun in the English grammar period, she used to – with some pride – translate them as *Isme Nakra* and *Isme Maarfa*. It was sheer exhibitionism.

She often talked about the good old days of Lahore when Hindus, Muslims and Sikhs rubbed shoulders with each other. But she gave Christian names to all her seven poodles, who came to school with her in a vintage Ford, driven by Habib, her orderly. While she was in school, Habib and the dogs moved around freely on the premises. Later she left all her wealth and her spacious bungalow to Habib. We left Lahore while she was still in harness, which is why I don't know if Habib did look after her poodles or simply sold them, for they would have fetched him a good price. As long as I was at the school, I remained her blue-eyed boy because thanks to the anglicized atmosphere in Bombay my command over the English language was better even than that of my seniors.

Strangely enough, English was hardly spoken in Lahore. Punjabi and Urdu were the only two languages one could hear – a far cry from cosmopolitan Bombay where so many languages were spoken. With the departure of the Hindus and Sikhs there were just Muslims left and some Christians, albeit in an insignificant minority. Many of the poorer Christians were sanitary workers and were discriminated against not because of their religion but because of their vocation. The Anglo-Pakistanis, particularly those with a fairer skin, enjoyed a privileged position. Most of them migrated to Australia, including the Rawalpindi-born Duncan Sharpe, a neighbour in Model Town, who played three Tests for Pakistan, all of them against Australia. As in India, the Anglos, as they were called, were largely employed by the Railways and even in the fifties the Railway Officers' Club in Karachi was dominated by the Anglo-Pakistanis.

I played with the Christian kids, whose parents lived in the servants' quarter in our bungalow. However, I couldn't rise above my linguistic limitations. They only spoke Punjabi and I couldn't understand the language. It took me a few months to be able to communicate with them and by that time I had made friends with children of my own age in the neighbourhood.

An insane and physically handicapped Sikh woman, who angrily cursed everyone, shouting '*Mur jao, mur jao, sare mur jao*' ('Die, all of you') at regular intervals, was left behind by the fleeing Sikhs. She had nowhere to go. A maulvi, who hailed from East Punjab, gave her food thrice a day. This pious man was the one who bore the brunt of her curses more than anybody else. 'Poor woman, she saw the killings and lost her sanity,' he would tell all those who questioned his wisdom in helping someone who abused him morning, noon and night.

Shalwar-kameez was the common dress among the ladies. Some refugee ladies who migrated from the Uttar Pradesh wore *gharara*, but sari was rare. My mother wore the sari both at home and outside. It is sad to see that this graceful dress has lost ground to *shalwar-kameez* even in the southern part of the subcontinent.

Kashmiri tea was a popular hot drink. Green tea was yet to arrive and black tea was taken only in winter. Our neighbours wondered how my parents could take tea twice a day twelve months in a year. Coffee, which was available even in modest restaurants in Bombay, was served only in classy and expensive restaurants. These days the beverage is served even in restaurants that cater to the middle class. As for tea, the per capita consumption in Lahore is now no less than in any major town in the subcontinent.

SETTLING IN KARACHI

In 1953, I moved with my parents and brothers to Karachi and for quite a few years I missed the open spaces of Lahore, its greenery and the incense that wafted from the trees and the bushes, not to speak of the glow-worms that flew lazily at night from one plant to another.

Shifting to Karachi was like a second migration. As the capital of the new country and its commercial centre, the city offered greater opportunities. My father was happy because his three brothers had established themselves fairly well there and my mother was glad because compared to Lahore, Karachi was more like Bombay. Geographically too it was nearer to Bombay than Lahore was.

But disappointment greeted us at Karachi railway station, where we learnt that a relative, who was a confirmed bachelor, and who had promised to share his flat with us till we found a place of our own, had backed out. One of my father's brothers and his generous wife came to our rescue. But the hunt for a house proved more difficult than the search for a job for my father.

In the end, both happened more or less at the same time. We found a small self-contained two-room house with a courtyard in a new colony on the outskirts of Karachi. It was called Paposhnagar (*paposh* means shoes) because the members of the society that built the colony had owned small shoe factories in North India, mainly Delhi, Agra and Kanpur. We paid Rs 25 by way of rent, almost 10 per cent of my father's salary. The owners occupied most of the houses; only a few were given on rent.

The menfolk had set up their shoe factories in Karachi on a cottage industry basis or had found employment in larger factories, while the women stayed at home – running the household and bringing up their many children. The ladies referred to each other by the cities they came from and in the case of those who migrated from Delhi the names of their *muhallas* were used as suffixes. My mother was called *Bumbai wali behan*. There was one lady from Jhansi and she was referred to as *Jhansi ki Rani* because about that time Sohrab Modi's movie by that name was doing good business in Karachi's Paradise Cinema.

The experience of moving from the upper storey of a large bungalow in Model Town – then the most posh locality in Lahore – to a quarter only slightly larger than the previous house's drawing room was heartbreaking. But my parents had prepared me and my younger brothers mentally for the unpleasant transition.

My mother became a friend, philosopher and guide to the simple ladies of the locality. She advised them to send their daughters to school and the girls proved to be better in studies than their brothers. Initially the idea seemed quite outrageous to the women in the family and more than that to the male folk. 'What nonsense, I don't want my girls to take up jobs. I want them to become good housewives like their mother and grandmothers have been,' was a common remark.

Some women agreed to send their daughters to our house, where my mother taught them basic English and Urdu as well as simple arithmetic, without charging them a fee. All those girls later joined the government school, a kilometre away from the colony. My mother taught embroidery to three or four women, who in turn tutored other females in their families.

My mother, soft-spoken and always helpful, became popular among the ladies. The elderly among them had one perennial complaint: 'You are such a nice woman,' they would say 'but your one major shortcoming is that you don't wear a burqa.' My mother would smile evasively and change the subject.

Initially we were very surprised when a lady would knock at the door and ask for a pot of sugar or a few onions – which were promptly returned at the first possible opportunity. In posh Model Town no such lending or borrowing relationship was even thinkable but the people in Paposhnagar were simple-hearted and naïve.

These women would often recall the towns they migrated from. A mood of nostalgia would overpower them. A couple of ladies lost no opportunity to curse the Hindus, who forced them to leave their hearths and homes in Delhi's Karol Bagh. My mother would then try to explain to them that some Muslims did the same in Pakistan. 'You would say that, because you came from Bombay and you didn't see your relatives being killed. You didn't leave your well-furnished house behind,' one woman once retorted, losing her temper and leaving for her home in a huff. The next afternoon she knocked at our door. She had come with a bowl of *halwa* that she had cooked for her sister who was visiting her from Hyderabad (Sindh). That was her way of apologizing for being rude to an ever-helpful person. The subject was not discussed again.

Unlike Punjab, Sindh did not witness rioting on a massive scale. There were just sporadic incidents and the Sindhis who left for India did so for better opportunities. In Karachi, I was told that when communal rioting broke out on Burnes Road, sometime in early 1948, Prime Minister Liaquat Ali Khan rushed to the site. He normally wore a *sherwani* but in his hurry he left in just kurta and pyjama. That reflected his sense of urgency. He mixed with the people in the locality and appointed a peace committee, which comprised young and old. He assigned the job of protecting the Hindus to a team of young Muslims, who I believe did a good job.

Roshan Lal Bhatia, an octogenarian I spoke to in Bombay recently, recalled how his mother who was the last family member to leave for India because she was waiting for the right price for the family restaurant, was escorted by the buyer and given the agreed amount in cash when she boarded the steamer for Bombay. 'Karachi was a peaceful city,' said Mr Bhatia, whose son Siddharth is a noted Bombay-based journalist. The junior Bhatia visited Karachi recently and saw the places his father refers to from time to time.

KARACHI TRANSFORMED

One of the most populous cities of the world today, Karachi is a far cry from the fishing village and fledgling seaport that Sir Charles Napier annexed in 1843 and brought under the control of the East India Company. Unlike Lahore and Delhi, it does not have a long history and a prosperous past. Even in 1936, when Karachi became the capital of Sindh, as the province was separated from the Bombay Presidency, it did not rank among the top five cities of undivided India.

The biggest and the swiftest change – demographic, linguistic and cultural – came with Partition. In Lahore and other cities of the West Punjab, the cross migration, though gigantic in scale, was not out of proportion. The Muslims who crossed into Pakistan were almost in the same numbers as the Sikhs and Hindus who left for India, which is why Lahore did not expand dramatically, for most refugees occupied or were allotted accommodation left vacant by the fleeing Sikhs and Hindus. In the peaceful city of Karachi, on the other hand, fewer Hindus left but a very large number of Muslims from different parts of India moved in, principally by two routes – from the Sindh-Rajasthan border and by sea from Bombay.

As a result, there was a great need for new houses. Large localities of thatched huts sprang up in a matter of months. The largest of these slums was around the mausoleum of the country's founder, Mr Jinnah, who was their *Quaid*, their leader. The refugees or Mohajirs, as they were called, were mostly from the Muslim minority provinces, where the demand for a separate homeland was raised. Ironically, a large number of such people were left behind in India. Equally sadly, some who didn't believe in the two-nation theory had to migrate, however reluctantly, or pay the price for Partition. Subsequent events proved them right. That the brunt of Partition was borne by the minorities on both sides (the Muslims in India and Hindus in Pakistan) is a fact now widely accepted.

The rehabilitation of the refugees was carried out efficiently by earlier governments despite the limitation of funds and the stupendous demand for housing. Guru Mandir (some people tried to change the name of the locality to Sabeelwali Masjid but failed miserably) was the last outpost of the city until 1947 but today it is very much a part of central Karachi. Malir, in the north, once a small town a few miles away from Karachi, has been devoured by the megacity.

Those living under thatched roofs were slowly, but very steadily, shifted to colonies where the governments, central and provincial, built up two-room quarters with independent kitchens, courtyards, bathrooms and toilets. Most of them had piped water connections; the remaining ones had community taps for a year or two before they too enjoyed water twice a day in their bathrooms.

Thanks to the liberal loans given by the House Building Finance Corporation at low interest rates, construction in Karachi was at its zenith from the fifties to the seventies. Had it not been for this government body, middle-class localities like Nazimabad and PECHS (Pakistan Employees Cooperative Housing Society) would not have cropped up within the first decade of Partition. Unlike Bombay, which has sea on its three sides, Karachi didn't grow vertically. It spread widely and wildly in three directions. Incidentally, on the fourth side is the Arabian Sea. Only in the late seventies did we get to see multi-storeyed flats, which again have largely been confined to four or five floors.

For a city which had to accommodate refugees almost twice its population in a matter of six months, the need for housing was stupendous. Corruption had not yet seeped into the bureaucracy, which was why modest quarters were built at an amazing speed in the fifties. General Ayub Khan's trusted lieutenant, General Azam Khan, got thousands of quarters built in Korangi, outside the city limits, in a record time of six months. All basic amenities were provided in the locality and a bus service was organized. Thus, the large slums that had erupted around the mausoleum of Mr Jinnah were cleared. Similar quarters, though on a smaller scale, were made in Orangi, in the north-east of the city. The construction boom attracted unskilled labourers from the Punjab and the North West Frontier Province (NWFP). By the sixties, the number of Pathans in Karachi was greater than in any city of the Frontier province, and that included the capital Peshawar.

Middle-class localities sprang up all over Karachi and in 1955 we moved to Nazimabad, where the residents were largely refugees from North India. Since South India was much less affected by communal disturbances, there were fewer refugees from the south, except Hyderabad, from where the migration started after the Indian army annexed the state in 1948. Shortly after that, Hyderabad Colony sprang up near the Karachi Central Jail, where you could get a wide variety of Hyderabadi pickles and other delicacies. During the month of Ramazan, many makeshift shops sold *harees*, a low-spiced version of *haleem*. But in all these years a round-the-year delicacy has been *bagharey baingan*. Later, the more affluent among the refugees from the Deccan pooled their resources to build Bahadurabad, a colony named after their leader, Nawab Bahadur Yar Jung.

Several colonies set up by refugees from different parts of India were named after those cities or provinces. For instance, there are three colonies that carry the name of the Indian capital – Dilli Colony is for the lower middle class, while Delhi Saudagaran Society and Delhi Mercantile Housing Society are both for entrepreneurs from Delhi. Then there are Benaras Colony, Kokan Society, CP Berar Society, Bantva Nagar, Kathiawar Cooperative Housing Society and Bihar Colony, to name the more prominent ones.

It was quite customary for people when meeting someone for the first time to enquire from which part of India they had migrated. If they belonged to the same city, the next question was about the locality where they used to live. All such conversations acquired a tinge of nostalgia. Favours were granted to each other.

Shops were named after the original cities of the shopkeepers. The trend changed after the sixties but Karachi has retained outlets like Benaras Silk House, Madras Jewellers, Ambala Sweets, Lucknow Chat House, Aligarh Bakery, and Pilibhit Oil Depot (not many Pakistanis and not all Indians would know the location of Pilibhit). Then there is a whole shopping area called Bombay Bazaar. But what is most surprising is that almost every locality has a Meerut Kabab House. These are clones of the original Meerut Kabab House that closed down a few years ago. Not all of them are owned or manned by those closely or even remotely connected with Meerut. I know of a Pathan, who had no clue where Meerut was, who tried to run a Meerut Kabab House. The kababs that he sold were closer to Peshawari chapli kababs than to the original kababs from Meerut.

Most of the migrants were from Uttar Pradesh and Bihar, which was why Urdu became the lingua franca of the city. Even people who came from other provinces of India (and later from other provinces of Pakistan) and settled in Karachi (except for the Pathans who lived in ghettos) learned to speak chaste Urdu. In the late forties and the fifties we heard different styles of Urdu in Karachi, from the crude Karkhandari dialect, spoken by the semi-skilled workers in the old city of Delhi, to the sing-song Hyderabadi style, which didn't suit the menfolk, for it was quite effeminate. But by the sixties the UP style Urdu was adopted by all Karachiites.

Ismat Chughtai, the famous Urdu short story writer who lived in Bombay, once told writer-lyricist Javed Akhtar: 'If you want to listen to pure Urdu, don't go to Lucknow, go to Karachi.' And, strangely enough, sometime in the late seventies, that great lover of Urdu took a flight and came to Karachi, even though he didn't know anyone here except for an old friend from Aligarh, Mohsin Zuberi. I met him at Zuberi's house the day he arrived and later introduced him to poets and literary figures. Akhtar returned to Bombay a week later, taking back some fond memories and leaving some behind.

Sadly, Urdu spoken by the later generations is not chaste enough. English words, of which there are simple substitutes in the national language, are unnecessarily included in the conversation. Deejays of FM Radio programmes and some television breakfast show hostesses, who are basically Urdu speaking, try to flaunt their knowledge of English by interspersing their conversation with English words. More recently, with the cable network showing Indian soaps, a few Hindi words have entered the day-to-day language too. But what is much more noticeable is the fast disappearing species of bilinguals, people who are equally at ease in the two principal languages of Karachi – Urdu and English. Until the eighties those who were well versed in both the languages were looked at with respect.

While on Hindi soaps, one can say that serials such as *Kahani ghar ghar ki* and *Saas bhi kabhi bahoo thi*, though thematically and treatment-wise poor and monotonous, showed television viewers in Pakistan that the people on the other side had the same culture and spoke more or less the same language. That to a very large extent made the viewers, particularly women who were initially addicted to the serials, realize that the people on the other side of the Great Divide were not all anti-Muslim and anti-Pakistan. The situation is reminiscent of the time when in the seventies and early eighties PTV's (Pakistan Television) serials, particularly those written by Haseena Moin, which were refreshingly different from Doordarshan's insipid serials, were widely available in the video parlours of North and Central India. Every week when an episode was aired on PTV, recordings were sent by the first flight to Delhi and Bombay, from where pirated copies were despatched to other stations. 'Look they dress up like us, they speak the same language and behave like us,' a Hindu lady who had never visited Pakistan told one of my cousins.

Initially the Hindus kept a low profile in the city but for the last two decades their presence has been much more pronounced. A number of Hindu doctors have moved from the interior of Sindh to Karachi for better job and practicing opportunities. Hindus are in a wide variety of professions, from architecture to fashion designing and from journalism to medicine. They are also into business. Then there is a small minority of Gujarati Hindus who are generally poor. The Dalpat-Kaneiria family has produced two prominent Test players and a few first-class players. Pak Hindus is a strong club team, which comprises only Gujaratis. Sindhis, whether Hindu or Muslim, don't play cricket. One of the very few Sindhis to play Test cricket was Karachi-born Ramchand, who played for India after he migrated from Sindh around Partition. The Test cricketers to emerge in Karachi have been either from families which migrated from India or who shifted to the metropolis from the Punjab.

REVISITING INDIA

A large number of people who migrated from Pakistan to India and vice versa have never managed to re-visit the cities of their birth but that has not been the case with me. My links have remained unsnapped. As a young boy, I visited Bombay with my parents, first in 1955 to see my ailing grandfather and the following year to attend the wedding of an uncle. But it was not until the summer of 1964, when I was studying for my graduation with honours in English literature at the University of Karachi and was at the same time editing *Eastern Film,* Pakistan's most widely circulated English language magazine, that I decided to go to Bombay on my own. The route that I chose was to take a train to Lahore, another to Amritsar and from there to Lucknow and Allahabad, before taking the long rail journey to Bombay. In those days there were no travel restrictions imposed by the Indians on the Pakistanis and vice versa. Unlike now, a Pakistani entering India by one route could take a different route for departure. I planned to return to Karachi by the familiar sea journey.

At that time, the Pakistan government issued two kinds of passports: one for India and the other, called an International Passport, for travelling to other countries. The latter was difficult to acquire. Later, when the government decided to include India in the International Passport one had to get a 'no-objection certificate' from the Ministry of Interior, which was relatively easy. The names of the countries one could visit were stamped on the passport. Later the formality of the NOC was dropped and the passport simply said: 'For travel to all countries except South Africa and Israel'. After the end of apartheid, the ban on travel to South Africa was lifted and the 'exception' clause was removed totally. Technically speaking, one can visit Israel too, but no one would like to take the risk. I have not known anyone who has visited there.

The train to Amritsar (it wasn't yet christened Samjhauta Express) was waiting for its passengers at a specially enclosed platform at Lahore railway station, known for its fort-like façade. After the immigration and custom check, I boarded a third class compartment (there was only one class on that train) and shortly before the train could steam out of the station, a middle-aged lady came with her old father, who could hardly walk with a stick. 'Will somebody help my father board the Howrah Mail at Amritsar and disembark at Shahjahanpur station?' enquired the lady. 'Someone who was to escort him has backed out and my father has to visit his ailing sister.' I volunteered to help the old man. A seat was found for him, much to the relief of the lady. She left the compartment when the train began to move.

The Pakistan railway police stepped out of the train as it halted for half a minute at Wagah station. It then moved slowly towards the international boundary. I looked out but, much to my disappointment, I couldn't identify the dividing line. The barbed wire was not to be fixed until the nineties. It was only when I saw Sikhs working in a field that I realized the train had entered India. At Attari the Indian police boarded the train before it raced towards Amritsar. The thought foremost in my mind was that there were no restrictions on birds and even stray animals crossing the man-made border. Seventeen years earlier the same railway track was smeared with blood.

As the train came to a halt at Amritsar railway station, passengers ran towards the immigration counters. With the elderly gentleman to escort, my progress was snail-like. I should have first rushed towards the counter, established a place in the queue and then brought the gentleman with me. But I was an inexperienced traveller on that route and had to pay a tough price for it. I was at the tail end of the queue. The old man was asked to sit on a bench. After an agonizing wait of two hours, by which time the Howrah Mail had left, I moved with my fellow traveller towards the customs section. The Sikh officer was nice but he did open all our steel trunks (suitcases were in those days used only by air travellers). 'Oh, you are a dangerous fellow, you read murder stories,' he quipped. The poor man didn't know the significance of T.S. Eliot's poetic drama *Murder in the Cathedral*, when he saw the slim volume.

By the time we reached Platform No. 2, the Sealdah Express, the second train that could have carried the old man to Shahjahanpur and me to Lucknow, had also steamed out of the station. I was told the next train to our destinations would not leave for another twenty hours. I was at my wits' end. Our coolie suggested that we board the Kalka Mail and change trains at Ambala and we were lucky to find ample space on the train. But for some reason it didn't leave Amritsar until forty-five minutes after the scheduled departure time.

As we got down from the train at Ambala Junction a few hours later, I was told that the connecting train had left on time but the Howrah Mail was expected. 'How come?' I asked the coolie we had engaged. 'Its engine failed at Ludhiana. It took four hours for it to be replaced. The Howrah Mail should be here any moment,' came the answer.

But my happiness proved short-lived. The train, when it arrived, was packed like a tin of sardines. I might somehow have entered a compartment but there was no question of the old man following me and, of course, we had our trunks too. There was no place for them. The coolie took me to the Attendant's Compartment, which was supposed to be for servants accompanying their masters travelling in first class. Railway policemen didn't allow anyone to enter the compartment. The coolie asked me to part with ten rupees, quite a sum in those days. He whispered something to one of the constables and then quietly slipped a ten-rupee note into the breast pocket of the cop and helped us board the train. The old man found a berth all to himself. Just as the guard blew the whistle, three college students forced their way into the compartment. One of them told the policemen that his father was a high-ranking officer in the railway and that any attempt to stop them would mean that they would lose their jobs. The trick worked.

In 1964, relations between the two countries were sour, even though the Pakistan foreign minister, Zulfikar Ali Bhutto, had dashed to Delhi to attend the funeral of Pandit Jawaharlal Nehru, who had passed away only a week earlier. I didn't want to reveal my nationality and, therefore, avoided conversing with the young men, who were only two or three years younger than me.

'What time did we leave Lahore?' the old man asked me, adding to my uneasiness. Before I could reply, one of the boys said: 'Oh, so you are from Pakistan?' I replied in the affirmative. 'You must have celebrated Panditji's death,' his friend commented.

'Well, we don't celebrate anyone's death,' I replied, 'and as for

Panditji, I respect him a lot for he was a great scholar. I read two of his books only recently.'

'What books? Did he write any book?' asked one of the boys, looking at his friends.

'Of course, he did,' I told him and went on to give an introduction to *The Discovery of India* and *Glimpses of World History*. The boys listened to me in rapt attention, as I spoke at length and quoted a couple of lines that were etched on my memory. I then told them about the rousing reception that their prime minister had received in Karachi when he came to sign the Indus Water Treaty. The boys turned into my admirers. One of them reminded me: 'You haven't answered Chachaji's question. Tell him what time you left Lahore.' I told him it was around 4 pm.

At the next station, whose name I forget, the boys bought *halwa-puri* for breakfast for their Pakistani fellow travellers and refused to accept money. Once when the old man wanted to go to the loo, the boys helped him. They also found a coolie for him at Shahjahanpur station. I was relieved when I saw a young man looking out for him at the station. He was his nephew. His mother was out of the hospital and was recovering, he told the old man, who hugged all four of us before we boarded the train again.

The railway policemen who replaced the earlier ones somehow found out that I was a Pakistani. One of them demanded money for boarding the Attendant's Compartment but my new friends gave him hell. 'Aren't you ashamed of demanding a bribe from a guest? What impression would he carry of us?' the one with a loud voice said. It was an emotional farewell that I got from my fellow travellers at Lucknow's Charbagh station. One of them offered to get me a rickshaw for Basant Cinema, which was close to my host's house.

I won't dwell on my twenty-four-hour visit to Lucknow, the four-day stay in Allahabad or the long train trip to Bombay's Victoria Terminus station. But returning to Bombay was fun. I got to meet some film people at a fund-raising function for the Anjuman-e-Islam High School, including Dilip Kumar. Later I interviewed the great composer Naushad for *Eastern Film*. A major attraction was to see some new Indian films. Import of movies from India was banned in Pakistan to give protection to the nascent local film industry, a step that proved counter-productive, as the plagiarists then had an open field. Some of the producers began sending their writers and directors to Kabul to watch the latest Indian films and they came back to write plagiarized versions of the movies they saw.

MAROONED IN BOMBAY

My link with Bombay was now quite strong and a year later I decided to take another trip, ignoring the fact that the time was inopportune. The Kutch conflict of early 1965 had died down, but in August the disturbance in Kashmir was taking an ugly shape. Thinking that it would end with a whimper, like it did in Kutch, I decided to go to meet my relatives and interview some celebrities for the magazine that I was editing in Karachi.

In the third week of August 1965 I boarded the *S.S. Sabarmati*, not knowing that it was to be my last voyage. The sea was unusually choppy but I had never suffered from seasickness so the tablets that my mother had put in my bag were offered to a couple of fellow passengers.

The officers manning the immigration and customs counters at the arrival shed of the Princess Docks in Bombay had an unenviable job, for as usual the ship brought more passengers than it was supposed to carry.

Film addict that I was, I began to see a movie almost every other day. I also tried to establish contact with the people I had met the previous year. A friend of my uncle's invited me to see the 'rushes' of the Dilip Kumar-Waheeda Rahman starrer *Dil Diya Dard Liya* at Kardar Studios. I was quite disappointed to see that Naushad, with whom I had spent an evening only a few months earlier, refused to recognize me. I was soon to learn that in view of the tense relationship between Pakistan and India, the Indian Muslims, particularly those who were in the public eye, were avoiding Pakistanis like the plague. But full marks to Dilip Kumar, who agreed to speak to me for two minutes. He said he would grant me an interview a fortnight later, as he was going to Madras to shoot *Aadmi*. In the brief conversation we avoided any reference to Pakistan; we just spoke about his under-productions. He was a bit taken aback when I remarked that after his excellent performance in *Ganga* Jamuna, there was really nothing left for him to achieve. 'Wait till you see my two new films, *Ram aur Shyam* and *Aadmi*. I would like to have your views then,' he said, sporting his winsome smile.

Four days later, on 6 September, after watching a movie in a cinema on Lamington Road, I went to see Naushad's brother, Irshad Ali, who was producing *Saaz aur Awaaz* and who was to give me stills from his film for publication in *Eastern Film*. There were three guests, all Punjabi refugees from Pakistan, in his office. 'Do you know your Ayub Khan has declared war on our country?' one of them said. I was shocked. They were quite rude, if not downright aggressive. Irshad Ali sensed trouble. He took me to the adjacent room on the pretext of giving me the stills, and asked me to leave. 'That's in your interest as well as mine,' he said.

Early editions of the evening papers carried screaming headlines: 'Pakistan declares War.' The newspaper vendors and the roadside stalls carried more copies of the eveningers than they normally did.

My uncle, with whom I was staying, had only two days earlier advised me to take the next ship to Karachi but I didn't take his advice seriously. Now I had to leave; there were no two ways about it. I went to report my exit at the nearest police station and was told that they were waiting for instructions but I could go to the airport and get the clearance from the immigration authorities.

At six in the evening one of my relatives tried to book a seat for me on the plane that was scheduled to fly to the Middle East via Karachi but we learnt, much to our dismay, that Karachi Airport was closed to civilian flights. The next day's issue of the *Times of India* carried a small news item that all air, road, rail and sea links with Pakistan were snapped. Alas, my friend the *Sabarmati* was never to sail to Karachi again.

There were fears that Pakistanis would be interned. In some cities, I was told that they were asked to report to the police station every day. I acquired an old suitcase and filled it with some books and my less favourite clothes, so that I could carry it with me when I was imprisoned.

The days were long and difficult to spend. My parents were worried about me. No letter or phone calls were allowed from India and vice versa. They feared that I had become a prisoner of war. There was no news of me and it was only after a month, through a family friend, who had British nationality and had flown to Karachi via London, that they learned I was staying with my uncle and not in a POW camp.

Everyone except close relatives avoided me. However, Zuleikha, a young lady, who had studied with me in Lahore and had four years earlier got married to a businessman in Bombay, gave me a lot of support. The couple often took me to clubs and restaurants. One day I was watching a movie with Zuleikha at Regal Cinema, when the film was interrupted by a slide, which said that there was an air raid warning. The audience was advised to go to the underground car park and the staff was supposed to guide us. But as it turned out, the staff was the first to run for safety. There was a rush for the exits. I didn't want to get stampeded so I convinced Zuleikha to be the last to leave the hall.

There were sounds of anti-aircraft guns, which to one of the ladies were thousand *ton* bombs. In those days the two combatants were trading charges of dropping thousand *pound* bombs on each other's civilian populations. Luckily, there was no truth in that. The film resumed once the ack-ack guns became silent, and when it ended, Zuleikha's husband was there to pick us up. He complained of traffic jams, not a common occurrence in Bombay of the mid-sixties. The next morning's paper carried the news of a couple of Pakistani aircraft that flew to Bombay on a reconnaissance visit. 'When our ground forces fired at the enemy planes, their pilots took to their heels,' is a sentence I can still recall from a local paper.

In Bombay there were no blackouts; there were what they called brownouts, which meant that the headlights of the vehicles were covered by brown paper and the lights in the buses and trains were switched off. Late one evening I found myself one of three passengers on the upper deck of a double-decker. The other two were Parsi men. They were sitting at the front, oblivious to my presence, while I was in one of the last rows. I heard one of them saying: 'These bloody Hindus and Muslims always fight with each other. As for me, I don't care if they kill each other but they should spare us. Now they are at war, we are in danger too. If a Pakistani bomb falls, it won't distinguish between a Parsi and a Hindu home.

Why should we be killed and why should our property be damaged? What have we done to Pakistan?' His friend agreed with him and said: 'Darius, I am thinking of migrating to England. I have had enough of this trouble.' I could see their viewpoint and didn't blame them.

A ceasefire was to be brokered by the US. Everyone was in a state of suspense. I was watching a movie in the morning and when the show ended, I saw much to my relief that the late morning daily, *Free Press Journal*, was carrying news of the ceasefire. I thought I would be on my way back to Karachi very soon. But that was not to happen. Every day the two sides accused each other of violating the ceasefire. The Tashkent Declaration was to take place four months later.

In the meantime, I decided to do something that I had been postponing for days. It so happened that before I left Karachi Miss Rhoda Vania, one of the associate professors at the University of Karachi, asked me to bring eye drops, which her old father got from Bombay. She told me to see a relative who worked for the Taraporewala Book Shop in Bombay. He was to arrange for the medicine. So after the ceasefire I went to see the Parsi gentleman, who was terrified the moment I told him that Miss Rhoda Vania had sent me. 'Oh, so you are from Pakistan,' he said, in a voice which betrayed his fright. 'No, I am from Karachi,' I said foolishly, thinking perhaps that Karachi was a less offensive name to utter. After all, the armed conflict was between Pakistan and India and not between Karachi and Bombay.

The next afternoon when I was at Zuleikha's place I got a phone call from my uncle who told me that someone from the CID office had come to take me to his boss. On reaching home, I picked up the old suitcase, thinking that I was finally going to be interned, when the man who was supposed to escort me said: 'Why are you taking your bag; we have no place for you to stay. All you have to take is your passport.' I was partly relieved. We took a bus and he paid for my ticket, saying that he was given money for our bus fare, but he clarified that he would not be with me on the return trip and that I would have to buy my own bus ticket then.

He took me to one Mr Takle, who was a junior officer in the CID office. Takle was busy writing notes on a paper. He asked me to sit down and resumed his work. I was quite tense but I couldn't have disturbed him. Once he completed his work, he filed the paper and put the file in a cabinet. Settling in his chair, he had a good look at my passport. Handing it back to me and taking off his reading glasses, he asked me why I hadn't gone to Poona when I had a visa for the city, to which I replied: 'Because of the unfortunate armed conflict between our two countries.'

'What do you think of the armed conflict?' Takle queried. I put all my debating skills to use when I gave a short speech on the need for peace between the two countries, which had millions living below the poverty line. Takle was taken aback and I suspect a bit amused. He said: 'OK, now tell me: why did you go to the Taraporewala Book Shop?' I was amazed. Miss Vania's relative must have gone to the CID office. I had nothing to hide, so I told the whole story to Takle, and added that if there were an embargo on my meeting the gentleman, I wouldn't go.

'I suggest you go and take at least two or three vials of eye drops, instead of one, for I don't see people from the two countries visiting each other in the near future. You can go wherever you want within the municipal limits of Bombay. Just keep away from the defence installations,' replied Takle. I was beginning to like the man.

'But where are the defence installations? How can I avoid them if I don't know where they are?' I asked. 'Oh, come on. Do you think I am an idiot? I won't tell you where they are because tomorrow if you are arrested you will state that I told you where the defence installations are. I too will be in trouble. You go and ask your relatives and they will tell you where they are.'

Takle began to like me too. After every third or fourth day, I went to him to find out if the circular allowing the stranded Pakistanis to leave had come from Delhi and he would assure me that it wouldn't take long. He offered me tea and puff biscuits from the nearby Irani restaurant. He told me that he would issue the exit permits when the Home Ministry issued a notification allowing the Pakistanis to leave. 'You will be the last man to get the exit permit,' he teased me. When he saw that I was visibly disturbed, he added: 'Don't worry! You'll be the first to get the exit permit. I want to get rid of you, the sooner the better, because you are a burden on my pocket. You demand tea and biscuits as if they are your birthright.' He then smiled from ear to ear. I still remember that.

But days passed and there were no signs of the exit permit. Two and a half months after the ceasefire, I heard that people with connections in the Home Ministry were getting special exit permits from New Delhi. I saw one ray of hope. I went to Mrs Fatima Ismail, who was my mother's godmother and a loyal member of the Congress Party. She had been close to Pandit Nehru and Indira used to call her Fatima Aunty. Baburao Patel, an extremist Hindu journalist, had once written about her: 'If there is one Muslim who can be trusted, then it has to be Fatima Ismail.'

Mrs Ismail gave me a patient hearing and was moved when I told her that my mother was very disturbed. She wrote a note to a senior officer in the Home Ministry, who answered to the name of Venkatesh. His office was at *Sachivalaya* (the Hindi name for Secretariat).

The next morning I met the man, who spoke with a clipped Oxonian accent. Bombay was not at all cold even in December but Venkatesh was wearing a lounge suit. Mind you, air-conditioning was not common in those days and neither was Venkatesh's desire to be a brown sahib.

He was cordial and correct. He asked me to take a seat and pressed the bell on his table. His secretary turned up with a pencil and a shorthand notebook in his hand. Venkatesh dictated a telegram (telex and faxes were to come in the seventies and the eighties) to the Secretary of the Home Ministry requesting that a special exit permit be given to me. He took my passport and ordered the secretary to send it by special mail along with the letter to Delhi. 'Cheer up young man! You should be on a flight to Karachi next week,' he said.

PIA and Indian Airlines were not operating but Alitalia and Air Ceylon had resumed their flights between Karachi and Bombay. Four days later I got a telephone call from Takle. He was amused. 'Where the hell are you? I am issuing exit permits to everyone and you are nowhere to be seen. Bring your passport immediately and go home. We have had enough of you.'

I told Takle that I had applied for a special exit permit because I wasn't getting it through the normal channels. 'You should have at least asked me before you did that foolish thing. Now you've had it. They will take their own time to return the passport to you. Go and see your Mr Venkatesh immediately,' he advised me.

I rushed to Venkatesh's office. Luckily, he was there. He called his secretary and asked him if my passport had been sent to Delhi. The man replied in the affirmative, so Venkatesh dictated another telegram asking the Secretary of Home Ministry to return the passport. 'You should get your passport in a couple of days,' he assured me.

I was disturbed, for I believed what Takle had said. When I stepped out of the office, I took out a packet of cigarettes from my pocket, offered one to the secretary and said that I didn't have a matchbox on me. The secretary opened his drawer and before he could pick out the matchbox, I saw my passport lying there. The man had forgotten to send it to Delhi. A perfect example of red-tapism, but it turned out for my good.

'Give me my passport,' I almost yelled.

'That's not yours,' the secretary said meekly.

'Show it to me; it's mine. If you don't, then I'll go to Mr Venkatesh and tell him that you didn't send the passport to Delhi. It's lying in your drawer. You'll be in trouble. So do as I tell you,' I said in a raised voice.

'OK, please don't speak loudly. Take the passport but promise me that you won't tell Mr Venkatesh,' he said sheepishly.

I did and I haven't broken the promise even after forty-three years.

Everyone was relieved that I was leaving. The hour and a half flight to freedom seemed to last till eternity. It was around 9 pm that I got to see the city lights of Karachi from the aircraft window. A Bombay paper had claimed that Karachi was still observing blackout, but thank goodness it wasn't.

I had decided that I would give a hug to the first Pakistani I saw. The man at the foot of the plane steps was shocked when he realized that someone he didn't know was trying to embrace him. He took a step backwards and the same moment it dawned on me that I was being too sentimental.

I was given a hero's welcome by my uncles and cousins, not to speak of my parents and brothers who had come to receive me at the airport. 'I won't let you go to Bombay again,' said my mother. I too was determined not to go back to India. At that point I thought it was too risky. And it was not until eleven years later that I stepped on Indian soil once again.

As I was not treated shabbily in India and I met some fine people such as Takle (sadly, I never got to see him again), I nursed no ill feeling for India. A well-known writer, now no more, invited me to meet his wife and children, with a view to narrating my tale of woes to them. He was disappointed when I told him that I moved around without any problem and saw some fine Bollywood movies.

The much needed peace agreement between India and Pakistan came with the meeting of President Ayub Khan and Prime Minister Lal Bahadur Shastri in the presence of Premier Alexey Kosygin of the Soviet Union. The Tashkent Declaration brought a whiff of fresh air to an atmosphere of war and hostility, but not without a tragedy. Shastri suffered a massive heart attack shortly after signing the Declaration on 10 January 1966. A picture published in the next day's *Dawn* showed Ayub Khan and Kosygin as pallbearers, shouldering the coffin of the Indian leader.

THE CAPITAL MOVES TO ISLAMABAD

Karachiites, as they are called, will never forgive the military dictator Ayub Khan for shifting the capital to Islamabad in the early sixties. The site of the new capital was close to his village Rehana and made him feel very much at home. When he removed the civilian government in 1958, he scrapped the plans to build a new capital at Gadap on the outskirts of Karachi.

When Mr Jinnah decided to make Karachi the capital of Pakistan, he thought everything went in favour of the city. It had a natural seaport, a full-fledged airport and a commercial centre. Lahore could have vied with Karachi but its location, a few miles away from the Indian border, was considered unsafe. In 1965, the Indian forces came perilously close to what has been described as the heart of Pakistan. Thanks to the BRB canal and a spirited fightback by the defenders, some of the Indian military officers' dream of having a *chota peg* in Lahore Gymkhana could not come true.

Ayub Khan loathed Karachi and some say disliked the mohajirs. 'Push them into the Arabian Sea,' he is reported to have once said at a party. One of the reasons for shifting the capital given by his supporters was that the bureaucrats ought to be kept as far away from the business class as possible to prevent them from getting corrupt. Sadly, this hasn't happened.

Ayub was destined to sign the Indus Water Treaty in September 1960 in Karachi, where the Indian Prime Minister, Pandit Jawaharlal Nehru, was given a rousing reception by the masses. He drove in an open car from the airport to the President's House in Central Karachi, as people lined both sides of Drigh Road (now Sharae Faisal) and raised slogans of Indo-Pak amity and '*Pandit Nehru zindabad*' (Long live Pandit Nehru). Earlier, when he walked out of his aircraft, he heard similar emotions expressed by the people who greeted him from the balcony of the airport.

The signing ceremony was followed by a grand public reception hosted in honour of the Indian prime minister on the sprawling lawns of Frere Hall, where he gave a memorable speech. I was a college student then and I remember that almost everyone wanted to shake hands with Nehru, who obliged as many as he could.

Despite Gandhi's assassination in Delhi and Liaquat's in Rawalpindi three years later, leaders in the subcontinent were not surrounded by security staff, not to speak of the presence of hordes of policemen, in uniform and in civilian clothes, which is quite the norm these days.

The venue of Nehru's meeting is now more or less out of bounds for the holiday crowd seeking fresh air, because on its two sides are the two most guarded places in the city, the American Consulate and the residence of the American Consul General. The US Consulate once had a public library and an auditorium where they screened American classics and documentaries, an invitation to which was not difficult to get. Today the consulate is out of bounds for the general public and those seeking visas have to fly to Islamabad for interview and finger printing. A large area has been earmarked for a new consulate on what was once Queen's Road, now Maulvi Tamizuddin Khan Road (named after the speaker of the first constituent assembly, who hailed from what was then East Pakistan). Once the new consulate is built, pressure on one of Karachi's main roads will be lessened somewhat, because two-wheelers, large vehicles, taxis and rickshaws are currently not allowed to ply on that strip.

RELATIONS WITH INDIA

Pakistan and India have always had a tit-for-tat kind of relationship, and until recently any effort to bring the two countries together turned into a 'one step forward, two steps backward' scenario. Hopes were raised when Rajiv Gandhi visited Pakistan during Benazir Bhutto's first tenure as prime minister. In the press conference they were both sugar and honey. We thought that hostility had become a thing of the past, but sadly it wasn't so.

The skirmish in Kargil was blown out of all proportions by the private television channels operating in India, which created a lot of bad blood. Doordarshan, the state-owned television channel, on the other hand, did not play to the gallery. The summit at Agra in 2001 proved to be a failure and the terrorists' attack on Parliament in New Delhi (later the same year) saw the relationship plummeting to a new low. In recent years, however, relations have greatly improved and communications between the two countries have opened up. Pervez Musharraf's decision to impose a ceasefire in Kashmir proved to be a big step forward in restoring peace at the Line of Control, and full marks to the Indian government for responding whole-heartedly. I have met quite a few people who lived in villages close to the LoC. Their movements were restricted and their houses pock-marked by bullets. They could not till their fields. The situation on the other side was much the same. No one could have imagined a few years ago that a bus service would carry passengers from Srinagar to Muzaffarabad and vice versa, even though not many people are able to use this facility. All passengers have to be vetted by the intelligence agencies on both sides and permission, even when it's granted, takes a long time.

Ill-feeling towards India is now almost non-existent, at least in Karachi, which has always had a love-hate relationship with the giant state next door. In the sixties and seventies, and even later, whenever I wrote about the need for friendship between the two countries, I was dubbed an Indian agent. I was warned that there would be a midnight knock some day. But mercifully there never was. Of late, however, a gentleman who lost no opportunity to call me an Indian agent has been visiting India almost every year with his wife and children, bringing back loads of saris and suit pieces. The grass is always greener on the other side of the fence: Indians visiting Karachi return with suitcases full of Pakistani cloth.

Sindhis, Baloch and Pathans have not had the same emotional relationship with India. To the Mohajirs in Karachi and other urban centres of Sindh, India is now a country their parents and grandparents came from. It's a country they would like to defeat at cricket, not on the battlefield. No one wants to fight. Happily, the Punjabis who always had a belligerent attitude towards India have mellowed down considerably – and that is not just the Punjabis living in Karachi but all over Pakistan. Whenever they meet Hindus and Sikhs speaking their language, a sense of camaraderie is developed immediately.

When I asked Sunil Gavaskar once in which city of Pakistan he felt most at home, he replied 'Karachi' without batting an eyelid. By the same token, Bishen Singh Bedi made it well known that he loved to visit Lahore more than any other place in Pakistan.

Sometime in the late nineties, when I was a member of the Pakistani delegation to a South Asian media conference in Delhi, the prime minister, Mr I.K. Gujral, had to be reminded by his aides at a lunch for delegates that there were journalists present from other SAARC countries. He had spent most of the time conversing with us in Urdu, mainly about his friend and mentor, the poet Faiz Ahmed Faiz.

At Gujral's luncheon, a distinguished looking gentleman from Allahabad asked me where I came from. He thought I was an Indian. I asked him to guess and he said: 'All that I can be sure of is that you are from UP.' I shocked him when I said: 'You are right I come from a city called Karachi.'

'What! Karachi is not in UP,' he blurted out. I replied: 'Well, if Delhi has become a Punjabi city after Partition, why can't Karachi become a UP city?' Sharmaji, as he was called by one and all, said that he would one day visit Karachi to verify my claim. I don't think the poor man got a visa because the vagaries of the relationship are such that you can only get a visa if you have relatives on the other side or if you have business relations.

Despite improvements in communication links, the fate of common people travelling to both sides of the border is unenviable. In Pakistan, the Indian High Commission has been more considerate than the Pakistani High Commission in India for the Pakistanis can send their applications along with their passports to the High Commission in Islamabad through a courier company but the Indians who want to travel to Pakistan have either to go to the High Commission in New Delhi personally or send someone to submit an application on their behalf and wait till the visa is granted or refused.

The problem doesn't end there because for one thing the nationals of both the countries get visas only for four to eight cities and, for another, they have to report their arrival and departure from each city at the local police station, which is too much of a hassle.

There is still so much of mistrust between the two governments that they have spurned suggestions of giving visas at the airports, railway stations and bus stops for those travelling by buses from Lahore to Delhi and vice versa. A Pakistani tourist or his Indian counterpart cannot cross the border.

What the MQM, the Karachi-based party with a strong Mohajir following, has been saying for ages, is that the Indian consulate, closed since the mid-nineties, should be reopened, at least for issuing visas, because more people in Karachi and Hyderabad (Sindh) have relatives in India than those living in other cities of Pakistan. But the Indian government's inability to provide accommodation to the Pakistani consulate in Bomay has stalled the matter.

The emergence of the MQM, initially known as the Mohajir Quami Movement, has helped to give a higher profile to relations with India. Led by Altaf Husain, once a student leader, who is now settled in London and pulls the strings from there, the party was later renamed Muttahida (or United) Qaumi Movement, but the acronym and the power base have remained unchanged.

When the MQM was formed in the eighties, many Mohajirs were happy that for the first time leadership had emerged from the middle class but sadly the party's following was confined to the urban areas of Sindh, where the refugees from India settled down. It could never attract the non-Mohajirs.

In the mid-1990s the MQM was in a state of war with the normalcy central government and for a number of years Karachi resembled a battle zone. Of late, however, normalcy has been restored, and the city government, which is run by the MQM, has done a fine job in improving the city. Roads have been resurfaced, flyovers, underpasses and bridges have been built and gardens have been laid out. The Musharraf government allocated generous funds to the city which generates most of the country's revenue and this enabled it to complete some badly-needed projects.

KARACHI'S COSMOPOLITANISM

Karachi is today the most cosmopolitan city in Pakistan, just as Bombay, now renamed Mumbai, remains the most cosmopolitan in India. If I were asked to compare the people of Karachi and Lahore, that other great city of Pakistan, I would say they have the same kind of rivalry that exists between Mumbaikars and Delhiwallas. Even before Partition, Karachi enjoyed the status of a cosmopolitan city – which Lahore has never had. There were far more languages spoken in Karachi than in Lahore. Sindhi, Urdu, Balochi, Brahvi, Gujarati, Marathi and Tamil could be heard before Partition, though Punjabi and Pushto have now replaced Marathi and Tamil. Currently there are more Pushto speakers in Karachi than in any other city including Peshawar, the capital of the Frontier Province, where Hindko, a mixture of Punjabi and Pushto, is also widely spoken.

Once it was a cultural shock for Pathans coming from the tribal areas to find girls in Karachi dressed in jeans and tops: now no more. But today there are a lot more young women covering their head and ears with *hijab*. That's the beauty of Karachi. Two active volunteers of Heritage Foundation, an NGO working on the restoration of heritage buildings, are journalist Shanaz Ramzi and fashion designer Shaiyanne Malik. Both are at ease in English and both work side by side, but while Ramzi covers her head with a dupatta, Malik wears sleeveless shirts and often goes out without a dupatta.

Heritage Foundation has developed a keen interest among school children and their parents in the need to preserve old buildings of merit. They were involved, for example, in cleaning the grimy surface of the red-stone State Bank of India building. Among the invaluable buildings restored in recent years are the fabulously designed Hindu Gymkhana and the architecturally stunning Mohatta Palace, which was built close to the beach shortly before Partition by Seth Mohatta. Partition followed and the building became an evacuee property. It now houses a small but scintillating museum.

In recent years Karachiites have become more art conscious. Almost every week there are one or two painting exhibitions in private galleries. More and more boys and girls are studying art and the most prestigious art school is the Indus Valley School of Art and Architecture, which is housed in its uniquely designed large building. A building in old Karachi, which was due to be demolished, was transferred brick by brick to the art school's campus, where it stands in its resplendent glory.

As bad luck would have it, television and videos have killed the theatre and more recently the cinema-going culture. Movie theatres have yielded place to shopping centres. Only one cineplex has been built in all these years, which is a far cry from Mumbai.

The most popular pastime with the people of Karachi is eating out. All major American fast food chains have several branches here. The malls have food courts but the barbecue joints, particularly the one in Clifton, attract more gourmets and gourmands.

Like Mumbai, Karachi has had its share of bomb blasts and has shown a great deal of resilience. In fact, Karachi was worse in the nineties when at one time people were reluctant to move out of the house at night because of sniper firing. Open air eateries had gone out of business. Who was behind it is not yet known.

Attempts were made to create a rift between the Sunnis and the Shias, the two main sects among the Muslims, when unknown people fired at the mosques of the two communities. Imambargahs, the worship places of the Shias, were also attacked by hit and run criminals, but ill-feeling between the two sects doesn't exist. The one good thing about the MQM, which has often rightly been accused of spawning violence, is that it has bridged the gap between the Sunnis and the Shias that was created by the militant mullahs in both communities. The members of the MQM are largely Urdu speaking refugees from both the sects, so there is no rift. It proves the point that I have been making for years that language is as great a bond, if not greater than religion in most cases.

The Ahmadis, declared non-Muslims during the Bhutto regime to please the mullahs, feel safer in Karachi than in the Punjab where they are in larger numbers. There are also more Christians, Hindus and Parsis in Karachi than in any other city of Pakistan, and all of them feel safe. They have prospered like the members of the majority community. As in most Indian cities, we find a growing middle class with disposable income.

Karachi is one city where very few people go to bed without a meal. There are eating houses, serving *nihari* (a meat curry), where poor people sit outside on the pavements waiting to be fed. We find people coming in cars and paying for the meals of ten, twenty or thirty people. In Ramazan a very large number of people are served food after sunset by some of the affluent families of the city.

If I were to describe Karachi city in one word I would say it is a compassionate city. A number of institutions for the welfare of the common people have emerged in this city, particularly in the field of health and education. They benefit the masses not only in Karachi but also in other towns of Pakistan.

One of these is The Citizens' Foundation, that runs over 450 schools of an educational standard close to, if not better than, most private schools. They are not only in Karachi but in towns and cities all over Pakistan and Pakistani administered Kashmir. Another is the Layton-Rehmatullah Benevolent Trust, which started with one eye hospital in Karachi and now runs as many as fifteen modern eye hospitals and thirty-nine eye clinics in different parts of the country. It is said that one out of three eye patients in Pakistan is treated at LRBT and one out of every four eye surgeries is done in these hospitals.

The Sindh Institute of Urology and Transplantation, a government hospital run by a dedicated team of doctors, does free surgeries and offers dialysis in small units all over the city. Relying more on donations than government grants, this institution has a huge state-of-the-art hospital building, which has a helipad on the rooftop to transport patients from outlying areas and nearby towns to the hospital, which is located in a densely populated locality of old Karachi.

Karachi is also the home of Abdus Sattar Edhi, who hails from the Indian province of Gujarat and is arguably the greatest philanthropist in the subcontinent. He runs homes where destitute women and unwanted children are housed. And at meal times large numbers of outsiders come to satisfy their hunger.

Edhi, who has been mentioned in the Guinness Book of Records for having the largest fleet of ambulances in the world, is an amazing person. He and his immediate family members run orphanages, schools, rehabilitation centres, hospitals, and hospices for cancer patients, not only in Karachi but in other parts of the country too. He picks up rotting bodies and gives them a decent burial. Karachiites wonder why this man has not been given a Nobel Prize for Peace, when people with lesser contributions have walked away with this honour.

When I compare Mumbai and Karachi, I sometimes feel they are twins that were separated at birth. The white-collar workers and the labour class in both countries make a beeline for these two great cities. It's a Gold Rush kind of a situation. The weather in both the cities is moderate, except that Karachi doesn't get even half as much rain as Mumbai, and both suffer from increasing congestion and pressure on services. Every time I go to Mumbai I find it more claustrophobic. The traffic, though more disciplined than in Karachi, drives me crazy particularly during the rush hour. When I visited the city in 2007, it took me an hour and a half to reach

South Mumbai from the airport with the result that I could not visit friends and relatives living in places like Bandra and Juhu, not to speak of more far-flung suburbs during my short stay.

Mumbai scores a major point over Karachi in its control of crime. There are occasional gunfights between Mafia groups in Mumbai but otherwise it is a city free from major crimes. Robberies are much less in number and cars are not snatched at gunpoint. The one plus-point that Karachi has is that you don't find people walking without shoes, nor do you see people sleeping on pavements. People sleeping on pavements in Mumbai are a sore sight.

Karachi and Mumbai have both been plagued by bomb blasts, but megacities as they both are, the unaffected areas continue to function more or less normally. Besides, they are both highly resilient. All said and done, there is no city in the world I love to visit more than Mumbai but if I am asked to choose between Mumbai and Karachi my vote will go to Karachi. In fact, after more than fifty years as a resident, I have come to feel about Karachi in much the same way as Milton wrote about England – 'With all thy faults, I love thee still.'